D0040808

THINGS
PRECIOUS
& WILD

THINGS
PRECIOUS
& WILD

A Book of Nature Quotations

John K. Terres

Fulcrum Publishing
Golden, Colorado

Copyright © 1991 by John K. Terres

Book design by Ann E. Green

Jacket photograph by Jeff Gnass
Copyright © 1991 by Jeff Gnass

Interior art courtesy of the Western History Department, Denver Public Library

The list of permissions for materials quoted is on pages 245–247.

Library of Congress Cataloging-in-Publication Data

    Terres, John K.
      Things precious & wild : a book of nature quotations / John K. Terres.
         p.   cm.
      Includes bibliographical references and index.
      ISBN 1-55591-072-6
      1. Natural history—Quotations, maxims, etc. 2. Nature—Quotations, maxims,
    etc. I. Title. II. Title: Things precious and wild.
    PN6084.N2T47   1990
    808.8'2--dc20   90-38239
                                                CIP

Printed in the United States of America

0 9 8 7 6 5 4 3 2 1

Fulcrum Publishing
350 Indiana Street, #350
Golden, Colorado 80401

To the men and women who wrote this book,
and speak to us here and now, of things without time;
and those who speak to us, here and now, from beyond the stars

TABLE OF CONTENTS

INTRODUCTION

I am a naturalist, former Editor of *Audubon* magazine, and an author, co-author or editor of more than fifty books of natural history. I am perhaps best known for my *Audubon Society Encyclopedia of North American Birds* (Knopf, 1980).

Besides reading widely in the scientific literature for that volume (4,000 references cited by author, title and publisher), I have for more than forty years kept a file of quotable lines from the writings of naturalists, scientists, and some poets and philosophers whose work I admired and loved. It seemed to me in my reading that some sentences, paragraphs, or whole pages leaped out of a book or article—precious ore that needed to be dug and held up for others to see. Not only had they charm and grace, but out of context they stood alone and told so much.

Ralph Waldo Emerson, American philosopher wrote: "people quote so differently: one finding only what is gaudy and popular; another, the heart of the author. ... The profoundest thought or passion sleeps as in a mine until an equal mind and heart finds and publishes it."

I selected mostly from authors who wrote about nature, who exalted the simple facts in a combination of wisdom, perception, and beauty. Often I went to my files to read and re-read them. All, to me, are memorable; many for the thoughts and poetic vision of the authors, some for brief but brilliant narrations of drama in nature. Others are remarkable for their clear exposition of those great principles that govern the lives of all animals and plants and that govern the lives of even ourselves. In a paragraph or two, an author may give us the tragedy of an animal or of a tree in its dying—the charm of a bird in its singing—or immerse us in wild places known only to the authors themselves. Some with the deftness of artists sketch the character of a wildflower or paint a rainbow such as we have never seen one before.

Later, I began to use some of these, in whole or in part, to illuminate and to strengthen a point in a book I was writing, or in an article for publication, or in a speech I was making.

Only recently did I think of the words and their authors as something I wanted to share more widely with others—a book of nature quotations, as inspirational to others as they are to me. I believe that this collection will create sympathy for wildlife such as no single author might inspire because it is a chorus—I am tempted to say "a wild chorus," for it is so—a body of appeal that is an assembly of philosophies and extraordinary observations of writers, so often different in their personal views, yet, all in profound agreement.

It is my dearest wish that the book will convince readers, in the words of Sir Winston Churchill, that "Quotations when engraved upon the memory give you good thoughts. They also make you anxious to read the author and to look for more."

Last, I think that this collection through the literary work of its distinguished—yes, even noble group of authors—is a powerful contribution to saving those things that, to so many of us are, and will remain, precious and forever wild.

John K. Terres
Bronxville, New York

THINGS
PRECIOUS
& WILD

ABBEY, EDWARD (1927–1989)

Author, novelist, naturalist, park ranger and
Fulbright Scholar (1951–52)

... I believe that there is a kind of poetry,
even a kind of truth, in simple fact. But the
desert is a vast world, an oceanic world, as deep
in its way and complex and various as the sea.
Language makes a mighty loose net with which
to go fishing for simple facts, when facts are
infinite. If a man knew enough he could write a
whole book about the juniper tree. Not juniper
trees in general but that one particular juniper
tree which grows from a ledge of naked sand-
stone near the old entrance to Arches National
Monument.

—Desert Solitaire:
A Season in the Wilderness

Poetry in Facts

A yellow planet floats on the west, brightest
object in the sky. Venus. I listen closely for the
call of an owl, a dove, a nighthawk, but can hear
only the crackle of my fire, a breath of wind.

The fire. The odor of burning juniper is the
sweetest fragrance on the face of the earth, in
my honest judgment; I doubt if all the smoking
censers of Dante's paradise could equal it. One
breath of juniper smoke, like the perfume of
sagebrush after rain, evokes in magical catalysis,
like certain music, the space and light and
clarity and piercing strangeness of the American
West. Long may it burn.

—Desert Solitaire:
A Season in the Wilderness

Sweetest Fragrance
on Earth

Emotions in Animals

I am not attributing human motives to my snake and bird acquaintances. I recognize that when and where they serve purposes of mine they do so for beautifully selfish reasons of their own. Which is exactly the way it should be. I suggest, however, that it's a foolish, simple-minded rationalism which denies any form of emotion to all animals but man and his dog. This is no more justified than the Moslems are in denying souls to women. It seems to me possible, even probable that many of the non human undomesticated animals experience emotions unknown to us. What do the coyotes mean when they yodel at the moon? What are dolphins trying so patiently to tell us?

—*Desert Solitaire:*
A Season in the Wilderness

The Seductive Prickly Pear

The prickly pear ... produces a flower that may be violet, saffron, or red. It is cup-shaped, filled with golden stamens that respond with sensitive, one might almost say sensual, tenderness to the entrance of a bee. This flower is indeed irresistibly attractive to insects; I have yet to look into one and not find a honeybee or bumblebee wallowing drunkenly inside, powdered with pollen, glutting itself on what must be a marvelous nectar. You can't get them out of there—they won't go home. I've done my best to annoy them, poking and prodding with a stem of grass, but a bee in a cactus bloom will not be provoked; it stays until the flower wilts. Until closing time.

—*Desert Solitaire:*
A Season in the Wilderness

Long enough in the desert a man like other animals can learn to smell water. Can learn, at least, the smell of things associated with water— the unique and heartening odor of the cottonwood tree ... which in canyonlands is the tree of life. In this wilderness of naked rock burnt to auburn or buff or red by ancient fires there is no vision more pleasing than the translucent acid green (bright gold in autumn) of this venerable tree. It signifies water, and not only water but also shade, in a country where shelter from the sun is sometimes almost as precious as water.

—*Desert Solitaire:*
A Season in the Wilderness

The Smell of Water

A man could be a lover and defender of the wilderness without ever in his lifetime leaving the boundaries of asphalt, powerlines, and right-angled surfaces. We need wilderness whether or not we ever set foot in it. We need a refuge even though we may never need to go there. I may never in my life get to Alaska ... but I am grateful that it's there. We need the possibility of escape as surely as we need hope; without it the life of the cities would drive all men into crime or drugs or psychoanalysis.

—*Desert Solitaire:*
A Season in the Wilderness

The Necessity of Wilderness

The Lovely Blue Columbine

The ascent of Tukuhnikivats has taken me half the day. ... On the way, in an area where spruce and fir mingle with quaking aspen, in a cool shady well-watered place, I discover a blue columbine, rarest and loveliest of mountain flowers. This one is growing alone—perhaps the deer have eaten the others—there must have been others—and wears therefore the special beauty of all wild and lonely things. Silently I dedicate the flower to a girl I know and in honor both of her and the columbine open my knife and carve something appropriate in the soft white bark of the nearest aspen. Fifty years from now my inscription will still be there, enlarged to twice its present size by the growth of the tree. May the love I feel at this moment for columbine, girl, tree, symbol, grass, mountain, sky and sun also stay, also grow, never die.

—*Desert Solitaire:*
A Season in the Wilderness

Strange Lure of the Desert

There is something about the desert. ... Even after years of intimate contact ... this quality of strangeness in the desert remains undiminished. Transparent and intangible as sunlight, yet always and everywhere present, it lures a man on and on, from the red-walled canyons to the smoke-blue ranges beyond, in a futile but fascinating quest for the great, unimaginable treasure which the desert seems to promise. Once caught by this golden lure you become a prospector for life, condemned, doomed, exalted.

—*Desert Solitaire:*
A Season in the Wilderness

ABBOTT, CHARLES C. (1843–1919)

Medical doctor, American naturalist, nature writer and archaeologist

One must not mope because he must stay at home. ... if the trees are not tall enough to suit your whim ... lie down beneath the branches of any one of them, and, as you look up, the topmost twig pierces the sky. There is not an oak but will become a giant sequoia in this way.
—*Days Out of Doors*

If the Trees Are Not Tall Enough

The world acquired a new interest when birds appeared for the presence of birds at any time is magical in effect. They are magicians that transform every scene; make of every desert a garden of delights.
—*Days Out of Doors*

The Magic of Birds

Poor persecuted crows! They have a hard time of it, and only their excellent wit has saved them from annihilation. I recently read of efforts to destroy a newly-formed crow–roost, and that the farmers of the neighborhood were divided into pro–corvites and anti–corvites. There is no need of coining a new word. Those who defend these birds are wise; those who persecute them, otherwise.
—*Days Out of Doors*

The Persecuted Crow

I am not willing to set all turtles down as fools. The cornered snapper shows he is not ... and I have knowledge of a box tortoise that recognized its keeper, and would come when he called it.
—*Days Out of Doors*

Turtle Intelligence

Advantages of Sitting in a Tree

What is to be gained by sitting in a tree? So much that my allotted space would not catalogue it. Rather, what is not gained? Cozily seated among beechen bough—are not those five words tantalizing to the toilworn folks of the cities, even in early July? Here is a gain not given to him who happens to be on the ground, even though sitting in the shade of some old tree. I find I am far less an object of suspicion, and the birds ignore me while I take notes of their pretty ways.

—Days Out of Doors

The Return of the Redwings

While I stand listening, there comes, borne upon the south wind, a faint tinkling note that thrills me more than all other sounds. It can not be mistaken for any other, and I know the redwings are on the way. Whatever the time of the year, there are joyful experiences in store for every rambler, but few that are more entrancing than to greet the crimson-shouldered blackbirds when they come in full force to the long-deserted meadows.

—Days Out of Doors

The Response of Birds to Beauty

Why, if the beauty that we recognize goes for naught among birds, does the grass-finch sing most sweetly during the few moments of a brilliant sunset? As I have passed over the upland fields at the close of the day, the sun has suddenly broken through the cloud banks on the horizon and filled the world with crimson and golden light. In an instant every grass-finch in the field mounts some low shrub and sings his sweetest songs.

—Days Out of Doors

Nature speaks freely to the individual, but seldom harangues a crowd.

—*Days Out of Doors*

ADAMS, J. DONALD (1891–1968)
Columnist, *New York Times*

The sense of wonder, which is the possession of every child, is the one soonest lost for most of us. Life both sharpens and dulls us, and the ways in which it sharpens us are commonly less admirable than advantageous. But if we cannot, unless we are lucky, keep the sense of wonder undulled, we can remember what it was like when pleasure, whether of discovery or of recognition, was so sharp as to approximate pain.

—*Speaking of Books and Life*

ALEXANDER, CECIL FRANCES (1818–1895)
English poet

All things bright and beautiful,
All creatures great and small
All things wise and wonderful
The Lord God made them all

—*All Things Bright and Beautiful*

ALLINGHAM, WILLIAM (1824–1889)
Irish poet and critic

Reverie

Four ducks on a pond,
A grass-bank beyond,
A blue sky of spring,
White clouds on the wing,
What a little thing
To remember for years—
To remember with tears
—*Four Ducks on a Pond*

ARISTOTLE (384–322 B.C.)
Greek philosopher, teacher, author
and classifier of animals in *Historia Animalium*

Birds

One swallow does not make a spring.
—*Nichomachean Ethics*

AUDUBON, JOHN JAMES (1785–1851)
Haitian-born American bird artist and naturalist

The Labors of My Life

I have spared no time, no labour, no expense
in endeavoring to render my work as perfect as it
was possible for me and my family to make it. We
have laboured at it, and every other occupation
has been laid aside, that we might present in the
best form the Birds of America to the generous
individuals who have placed their names on my
subscription list. I shall rejoice if I have in any
degree advanced the knowledge of so delightful a
study as that which has occupied the greater part
of my life. ...
—*Preface, Birds of America*

A vivid pleasure shone upon those early days of my youth. ... I gazed in ecstasy upon the pearly and shining eggs as they lay embedded in the softest down ... I was taught to look upon them as flowers yet in the bud. ...

—*Introductory Address, Vol. I*
Ornithological Biography

Loveliness of Birds' Eggs

The ornithology of the United States may be said to have been commenced by Alexander Wilson, whose premature death prevented him from completing his labours. It is unnecessary for me to say how well he performed the task which he had imposed upon himself; for all naturalists, and many who do not aspire to the name, acknowledge his great merits.

—*Preface, Birds of America*

Audubon's Salute to Wilson

The productions of nature soon became my playmates. I felt that an intimacy with them not consisting of friendship, merely, but bordering on frenzy, must accompany my steps through life. ...

—*Introductory Address, Vol. I*
Ornithological Biography

Audubon's Frenzy

AUDUBON, MARIA R. (?–1925)

Granddaughter of John James Audubon and editor of *Audubon and His Journals*

The Wastrel

Audubon drew, fished, hunted, and rambled in the woods to his heart's content, but to his purse's depletion. He describes his life in the episode 'Fishing in the Ohio,' and in these rushing present times (of 1900) such an Arcadian existence seems impossible. Small wonder that his wife's relatives, with their English thrift, lost patience with him, could not believe he was aught but idle, because he did not work their way. I doubt not many would think as they did, that he wasted his days, when in truth he was laying up stores of knowledge which later in life brought him a rich harvest. Waiting times are always long, longest to those who do not understand the silent inner growth that goes on and on, yet makes no outward sign for months and even years as in the case of Audubon.

—*Audubon and His Journals*, Vol. I

AUTHORS UNKNOWN

The young pine knows the secrets of the ground
The old pine knows the stars.

The Knowledge of Pines

    It depends on those who pass, whether I am
a tomb or a treasure, whether I speak or I am
silent.
    *—Inscription over the entrance to a Paris museum
on Maurice Chevalier's TV program,
March 6, 1957*

*What Nature and Art
Say to Us*

    Man is constantly adding to his knowledge
of the world, but to do any good it must be
shared—by the people.
    *—Advertising words by Xerox,
spoken by Alistaire Cook on
TV program, January 23, 1973*

*Knowledge
Must Be Shared*

Sitting still and wishing
Makes no person great
The good Lord sends the fishing
But you must dig the bait
    *—Quoted by John Masefield in
"The Best Advice I Ever Had,"*
The Saturday Review of Literature,
March 20, 1954

Wishing While Fishing

In the beginning water covered the Earth
and all creatures lived in the under world below.
People could talk, animals could talk,
rocks could talk.
    —Jicarilla Apache Tradition

Creation

BALZAC, HONORE DE (1799–1850)
French novelist

Laws of Art,
Laws of Life

Constant toil is the law of art, as it is of life.
—*Guides to Living*

BARTHOLIN, THOMAS (dates unknown)
Danish scholar

Our Need for Books

Without books, God is silent, justice dormant, natural science at a standstill, philosophy lame, letters dumb, and all things in Cimmerian darkness.
—*Quoted and circulated by*
New York Times Book Review

BARTRAM, WILLIAM (1739–1823)
American naturalist, traveler, collector of plants in early America and botanist

A Difference Between a
Plant and an Animal

The most apparent difference between animals and vegetables is, that animals have the powers of sound, and are locomotive, whereas vegetables are not able to shift themselves from the places where nature has planted them. ...
—*The Travels of William Bartram*

I am sensible that the general opinion of philosophers has distinguished ... the brute creature from ... mankind, by an epithet which implies a mere mechanical impulse, ... this we term instinct, which faculty we suppose to be inferior to reason in man. ... The parental and filial affections seem to be as ardent, their sensibility and attachment as active and faithful, as those observed in human nature.

—*The Travels of William Bartram*

Animal Instinct and Human Reason

The alligator when full grown is a very large and terrible creature, and of prodigious strength ... and swiftness in the water. I have seen them twenty feet in length, and some are supposed to be twenty-two or twenty-three feet. ... The head of a full grown one is about three feet, and the mouth opens nearly the same length. ... when they clap their jaws together it causes a surprising noise ... and may be heard at a great distance.

But what is yet more surprising ... is the incredible loud and terrifying roar, which they are capable of making especially in the spring season, their breeding time. It most resembles very heavy distant thunder ... causing the earth to tremble; and when hundreds and thousands are roaring at the same time, you can scarcely be persuaded, but that the whole globe is violently and dangerously agitated.

—*The Travels of William Bartram*

The Formidable Alligator

The Snake Bird

Here is and in the waters all over Florida, a very curious and handsome species of birds, the people call them Snake Birds. ... They delight to sit in little peaceable communities on the dry limbs of trees, hanging over the still waters. ... when we approach them, they drop off the limbs into the water as if dead, ... at a vast distance, their long slender head and neck only appear, and have very much the appearance of a snake. ... if this bird has been an inhabitant of the Tiber in Ovid's days, it would have furnished him with a subject for some beautiful and entertaining metamorphoses.

—*The Travels of William Bartram*

The Majestic Cypress Tree

The Cupressus disticha stands in the first order of North American trees. Its majestic stature is surprising; and ... we are struck with a kind of awe, at beholding the stateliness of the trunk, lifting its cumbrous top toward the skies ... a grand straight column eighty or ninety feet high, when it divides ... into an extensive flat horizontal top ... where eagles have their secure nests and cranes and storks their temporary resting-places. ... Paroquets are commonly seen hovering and fluttering on their tops, its seed being their favorite food.

—*The Travels of William Bartram*

I have in the course of my travels in the Southern states ... stept unknowingly so close as almost to touch one of them with my feet. ... But, however incredible it may appear, the generous ... creature lay still and motionless. ... I precipitately withdrew, unless when I have been so shocked ... as to be ... rivetted to the spot, ... when he slowly ... moves off ... unless pursued, when he erects his tail ... and gives ... warning. ... his head and neck are flattened, his cheeks swollen and his lips constricted, discovering his mortal fangs; his eyes red ... yet never strikes unless sure of his mark.
                    —*The Travels of William Bartram*

The "Generous" Rattlesnake

However attentive and observant the ancients were ... they seem to have been very ignorant ... concerning what becomes of birds, after their disappearance, until they return again. In the southern and temperate climates some imagined they went to the moon; in the northern regions they supposed that they retired to caves and hollow trees, ... where they remained in a dormant state ... and even at this day, very celebrated men have asserted that swallows at the approach of winter, voluntarily plunge into lakes and rivers, descend to the bottom ... where they continue in a torpid state, until the returning summer warms them again into life; when they rise, return to the surface of the water, immediately take wing, and again people the air.
                    —*The Travels of William Bartram*

The Ancients and Bird Migration

Learn Wisdom and Understanding from Nature

We are all of us, subject to crosses and disappointments, but more especially the traveller, ... but let us rely on Providence, and ... learn wisdom and understanding in the economy of nature, and be seriously attentive to the divine monitor within.

—*The Travels of William Bartram*

BATES, HENRY WALTER (1825–1892)
English naturalist and writer

We often read, in books of travels, of the silence and gloom of the Brazilian forests. They are realities, and the impression deepens on a longer acquaintance. The few sounds of birds are of that pensive or mysterious character which intensifies the feeling of solitude rather than imparts a sense of life and cheerfulness. Sometimes, in the midst of the stillness, a sudden yell or scream will startle one; this comes from some defenceless fruit-eating animal, which is pounced upon by a tiger-cat or stealthy boa-constrictor. Morning and evening the howling monkeys make a most fearful and harrowing noise, under which it is difficult to keep up one's buoyancy of spirit. The feeling of inhospitable wildness which the forest is calculated to inspire, is increased tenfold under this fearful uproar. Often, even in the still hours of midday, a sudden crash will be heard resounding afar through the wilderness, as some great bough or entire tree falls to the ground. There are, besides, many sounds which it is impossible to account for. I found the natives generally as much at a loss in this respect as myself. Sometimes a sound is heard like the clang of an iron bar against a hard, hollow tree, or a piercing cry rends the air; these are not repeated, and the succeeding silence tends to heighten the unpleasant impression which they make on the mind.

—*The Naturalist on the River Amazons*

Sounds in the Forest

Jungle Noises at Night

The whirring of cicadas; the shrill stridulation of a vast number and variety of field crickets and grasshoppers, each species sounding its peculiar note; the plaintive hooting of tree frogs—all blended together in one continuous ringing sound—the audible expression of the teeming profusion of Nature. As night came on, many species of frogs and toads in the marshy places joined in the chorus: their croaking and drumming, far louder than anything I had ever before heard … added to the other noises, created an almost deafening din. This uproar of life, I afterwards found, never wholly ceased, night or day: in course of time I became, like other residents, accustomed to it. It is, however, one of the peculiarities of a tropical—at least, a Brazilian-climate which is most likely to surprise a stranger. After my return to England the death-like stillness of days in the country appeared to me as strange as the ringing uproar did on my first arrival at Pará.

—*The Naturalist on the River Amazons*

BATES, MARSTON (1906–1974)
American biologist, writer and medical ecologist

Charles Elton has remarked that there is little use in making observations of an animal unless you know its name. The first step in a survey of natural history ... should be ... familiarity with the system of names and the system of classification, with the word equipment used by naturalists.

—*The Nature of Natural History*

Biological nomenclature is the invention of Carolus Linnaeus. I have just looked him up in the encyclopedia, and find that he gets slightly less than a column of biography. It is curious to find that the author of one of the great achievements of the human mind gets so little attention. On looking further, I find that Isaac Newton, surely one of the greatest of men, gets only half the space of David Lloyd George. It isn't specific neglect of Linnaeus: it is lack of general interest in the biographies and characters of the men responsible for modern science.

—*The Nature of Natural History*

The Names of Animals

Our Neglected Scientists

BEEBE, CHARLES WILLIAM (1877–1962)

American scientist, ecologist, explorer and writer; first winner of the John Borroughs Medal for *Pheasants of the World* (1926)

To Be a Good Naturalist

The joys of exploration are as varied as the numbers and characters of the explorers themselves, and the joys change during the lifetime of each person. I can remember when my greatest ambition was to be the first to step upon some tropical desert island, or to penetrate to where no white man's foot had ever trod. Then came the period of peripatetic journeys, of covering as much ground as possible in a given time. But I soon found that the island might be "desert" in every truth with no return in scientific loot, and the thrill soon passed of encircling a sandy spit and seeing none but one's own footprints. I came to learn that worthwhile observations of birds and animals and insects were great in proportion to the smallness of territory covered. One might shoot a large parrot or catch a brilliant butterfly as one travelled, but to go slowly or to sit quietly was to invite the acquaintanceship of many rare and interesting creatures. To be a good naturalist one must be a stroller or a creeper, or better still a squatter in every sense of the word. ...
—*Nonsuch: Land of Water*

The Charm of Pet Vultures

Some day I shall dilate upon vultures as pets—being surpassed in cleanliness, affectionateness and tameness only by baby bears, sloths, and certain monkeys.

—*Jungle Days*

To write honestly and with conviction anything about the migration of birds, one should oneself have migrated.

In historical times I seem to associate the first conscious thought of migrating birds with astrologers and the absence of sloping roofs. From the earliest times in the Far East men liked to sleep or to study the stars on the flat tops of their houses, and many an abstruse calculation of star portents of war ... must have been interrupted by the loud chirps of passing birds. Even this I have verified for myself. ...

One fortunate night I was permitted a glimpse of these vast flocks. I squatted on the swaying floor of the torch of the Statue of Liberty when the fog drifted in from the sea and closed down gray and silent. With it came birds which before had been only disembodied voices, and the fog, which obliterated the heavens and the earth, made the migrating flocks visible to my eyes. More and more they came, until a swarm of golden bees was the only simile I could think of. I dared not face them full, for now and then one struck the light with terrific impact. So I peered from behind the railing and watched the living atoms dash into view, shine for an instant, and vanish, so rapidly that when I looked through half-closed lids the driving sparks consolidated and lengthened into luminous lines. I think that I enjoyed it as a spectacle more in retrospect than at the time, for my emotion was distracted by the occasional thud at my feet of blackpolls and other warblers. It seemed such a cruel thing that even one of these lives which had been hatched and fed with such care in Hudson Bay or Labrador should be needlessly snuffed out because of the glare through a bit of glass.

—*Nonsuch: Land of Water*

Bermuda Rainbow

... high overhead there was etched the strongest, most materialistic rainbow I have ever seen, one end of which began in mid-air, and the other curved down, down, down, holding true from red to violet, to the rocks beside me. Once before, on a Guiana jungle river, I have been actually at the end of a rainbow, when, at my very side, one colored the bulwarks of our Akawai canoe.

—*Nonsuch: Land of Water*

Nature's Daily Toll of Life

Somewhere today a worm has given up existence, a mouse has been slain, a spider snatched from the web, a jungle bird torn sleeping from its perch; else we should have no song of robin, nor flash of reynard's red, no humming flight of wasp, nor grace of a crouching ocelot. In tropical jungles, in Northern home orchards, anywhere you will, unnumbered activities of bird and beast and insect require daily toll of life.

—*Jungle Days*

Leaf Song

Fallen leaves have a wind song all their own which is to be heard only when listened for consciously. When a fitful breeze is blowing, if the ear is held close to the ground, a low intermittent clatter and shuffling is audible, with occasionally a real rustle as a delicately balanced leaf is blown over. Stand up and the carpet of dead leaves becomes silent, their gentle talk lost in the hubbub of living, moving foliage.

—*Jungle Days*

A Fallen Tree

Nothing is more pitifully out of place than a fallen tree. It is like a floundered, deserted ship with decks awash, covered with a maze of broken masts, remnants of sails, and tangled rigging. ... the final surrender was at the demand of one of the natural elements, whose brothers had brought the tree into being and nourished it into maturity, a stroke of lightning, sister of the sun, the rain and the winds.

Down it had come, straight to the north and cut for itself a mighty glade. All other trees in its path, all stumps and saplings had gone down with it, and where for centuries had been dimness was now clear sunlight and a great expanse of open sky. The surrounding trees leaned far outward as if looking down with some strange arboreal sympathy for their fallen comrade.

—*Jungle Days*

Hearing in Wild Animals

We do not realize the acuteness of hearing of wild animals until we try to stalk them over dry leaves. A giant leaf may crash down from branch to branch and never cause a curassow or deer to start. I have seen a labba feeding in late afternoon under a nut tree when a whole branch with clusters of dead leaves hurtled to earth a few yards away, and the big, spotted rodent merely glanced up, casually munching as it looked. My next step slipped an inch sideways and crumbled a tiny leaf crust and without a second's investigation the animal gave one terrified squeal and fled headlong.

—*Jungle Days*

The Graceful Solitary Wasp

About a slender-waisted, quick-moving solitary wasp there seems to be always something of the exquisite courtier, a D'Artagnan of sorts, both insect and man equally deft and skillful in the use of their rapiers.

—*High Jungle*

The Marsh

The marsh, to him who enters it in a receptive mood, holds, besides mosquitoes and stagnation, melody, the mystery of unknown waters, and the sweetness of Nature undisturbed by man.

—*Log of the Sun*

Birding for the Beginner

No time is more propitious or advisable for the amateur bird lover to begin his studies than the first of the year. Bird life is now reduced to its simplest terms in numbers and species, and the absence of concealing foliage, together with the usual tameness of winter birds, makes identification an easy matter.

—*Log of the Sun*

The Excitement of Exploration

On a trip of exploration ... there are three phases of interest and excitement—anticipation, realization, and retrospection. ... But there is one single moment which is never quite duplicated. This is the moment when the first specimen is secured.

—*Galapagos: World's End*

The Sad Thing About Being a Hero

One sad thing about a hero is the difficulty of being continuously heroic.

—*Galapagos: World's End*

A photograph moves one less than a painting, so a word description can hope to succeed only by its very imperfections—with vast gaps and hiatuses to be filled by the imagination of the reader.
—*Galapagos: World's End*

The Inadequacy of Words

A first walk in any new country is one of the things which makes life on this planet worth being grateful for. ...
—*Galapagos: World's End*

First Walk in a Strange Country

And the next time you raise your gun to needlessly take a feathered life, think of the marvellous little engine which your lead will stifle forever; lower your weapon and look into the clear bright eyes of the bird whose body equals yours in physical perfection, and whose tiny brain can generate a sympathy, a love for its mate, which in sincerity and unselfishness suffers little when compared with human affection.
—*The Bird: Its Form and Function*

Compassion for Birds

BELT, THOMAS (1832–1878)
English geologist, naturalist and explorer

If happiness consists in the number of pleasing emotions that occupy our mind—how true is it that the contemplation of nature, which always gives rise to these emotions, is one of the great sources of happiness.
—*Introduction to The Naturalist in Nicaragua*

Nature and Happiness

BESTON, HENRY (1888–1968)
American writer and contributing editor to
Audubon magazine

On Being Alone

It is not good to be too much alone, even as
it is unwise to be always with and in a crowd. ...
—*The Outermost House*

Sea Horses

The long miles of beach are never more
beautiful than when waves are rolling in fighting a strong breeze. Then do the breakers
actually seem to charge the coast. As they
approach, the wind meets them in a shock of
war, the chargers rear but go on, and the wind
blows back their manes. North and south, I
watch them coursing in, the manes of white, sun
brilliant spray streaming behind them. ... Sea
horses do men call such waves on every coast of
the world.
—*The Outermost House*

To See the Night Sky

To see the night sky in all its divinity of
beauty, the world beneath it should be lovely,
too, else the great picture is split in halves
which no mind can ever really weld into a unity
of reverence.
—*The Outermost House*

Insect Symphony

... we are not sufficiently grateful for the
great symphony of natural sound which insects
add to the natural scene; ... all those little
fiddles in the grass, all those cricket pipes, those
delicate flutes, are they not lovely beyond words
when heard in midsummer on a moonlight
night? ...
—*The Outermost House*

When one has not spoken to another human being for twenty-four hours, a little conversation is pleasant exercise ... even the simple idiom, "Come in," may take on a quaint air of being breathless and voluble.

Conversation —
A Pleasant Exercise

—*The Outermost House*

... Winter is no mere negation, no mere absence of summer; it is another and a positive presence, and between its ebbing and the slow, cautious in-flow of our northern spring there is a phase of earth emptiness, half real, perhaps, and half subjective. A day of rain, another bright week, and all earth will be filled with the tremor and the thrust of the year's new energies.

Earth Emptiness

—*The Outermost House*

The world of today is sick to its thin blood for lack of elemental things, for fire before the hands, for water welling from the earth, for air, for the dear earth itself underfoot.

A Lack of
Elemental Things

—*The Outermost House*

When the Pleiades and the wind in the grass are no longer a part of the human spirit ... man becomes ... a kind of cosmic outlaw, having neither the completeness and integrity of the animal, nor the birthright of a true humanity.

The Cosmic Outlaw

—*The Outermost House*

It is not easy to live alone, for man is a gregarious creature; especially in his youth, powerful instincts offer battle to such a way of life, and in utter solitude odd things may happen to the mind.

Effects of Solitude

—*The Outermost House*

Fear of Night

Our fantastic civilization has fallen out of touch with many aspects of nature, and with none more completely than with night. ... With lights and ever more lights, we drive the holiness and beauty of night back to the forests and the sea; the little villages, the crossroads even, will have none of it. Are modern folk, perhaps, afraid of night? Do they fear that vast serenity, the mystery of infinite space, the austerity of stars? ...

—*The Outermost House*

Learn to Reverence Night

Learn to reverence night and to put away the vulgar fear of it, for, with the banishment of night from the experience of man, there vanishes as well a religious emotion, a poetic mood, which gives depth to the adventure of humanity.

—*The Outermost House*

To Sow Life

Suddenly on chancing to look bay-ward, I saw a small school of "herring." ... There were, perhaps, fifty or a hundred fish ... unable to enter the pond in which they were born, barred from it by a dam of Nature's making. As I stood looking off to the baffled creatures, ... I began to reflect on Nature's eagerness to sow life everywhere, to fill the planet with it, to crowd with it the earth, the air, and the seas. ... That immense, overwhelming, relentless, burning ardency of Nature for the stir of life! And all these her creatures, ... what travail, what hunger and cold, what bruising and slow-killing struggle will they not endure to accomplish the earth's purpose?

—*The Outermost House*

... Far out at sea, in the northeast and near the horizon, is a pool of the loveliest blue I have ever seen here—a light blue, a petal blue, blue of the emperor's gown in a Chinese fairy tale. If you would see waves at their best, come on such a day, when the ocean reflects a lovely sky, ...
—*The Outermost House*

Ocean and Sky

... Poetry is as necessary to comprehension as science. It is as impossible to live without reverence as it is without joy.
—*The Outermost House*

Poetry and Science

The three great elemental sounds in nature are the sound of rain, the sound of wind in a primeval wood, and the sound of outer ocean on a beach. I have heard them all, and of the three elemental voices, that of ocean is the most awesome, beautiful and varied. ...
—*The Outermost House*

The Great Voices of Nature

A year indoors is a journey along a paper calendar; a year in outer nature is the accomplishment of a tremendous ritual.
—*The Outermost House*

A Year Indoors and Out

Living in outer nature keeps the senses keen, and living alone stirs in them a certain watchfulness.
—*The Outermost House*

To Keep the Senses Keen

Nature is a part of our humanity, and without some awareness and experience of that divine mystery, man ceases to be man.
—*The Outermost House*

Man Without Nature

The Tracks of Birds

On the floors of sand, on ... slopes, I find patterns made by the feet of visiting birds. ... There is always something poetic and mysterious to me about these tracks in the pits of the dunes; they begin at nowhere, sometimes with the faint impression of an alighting wing, and vanish as suddenly into the trackless nowhere of the sky.

—*The Outermost House*

Unity of the Flock

... Into the bright, vast days I go, ... putting up sanderlings and sandpipers, ringnecks and knots, plovers and killdeer, coveys by the dozen, little flocks, great flocks. ... Yet it is no confused and careless hordes through which I go, but an army. Some spirit of discipline and unity has passed over these countless little brains, waking in each flock a conscious sense of its collective self. ...

—*The Outermost House*

Curlews Calling

... the curlews rose from close beside the inundated road, and, circling, called to other curlews; I could hear ... the clear reply. And then there would be silence, and I would hear the sound of autumn and the world, and perhaps the faint withdrawing roar of ocean beyond the dunes. ...

—*The Outermost House*

Whistling Wings

... The sound of a pair of "whistler" ducks on the wing is a lovely, mysterious sound. ... It is ... a clear sibilant note which increases as the birds draw near, and dies away in the distance like a faint whistling sigh.

—*The Outermost House*

... no one really knows a bird until he has seen it in flight.

—*The Outermost House*

The Tameness of Gulls

It is low tide and the herring gulls ... are feeding on the flats and gravel banks. As I watch them ... they seem as untroubled as fowls on an inland farm. Their talkative groups and gatherings have a domestic look. ... So accustomed to man have they grown, and so fearless, that they will follow in his very footsteps for a chance to scavenge food; I have seen the great birds walking round clammers who threw broken clams to them as they might throw scraps of meat to kittens. ...

—*The Outermost House*

The Clamor of Wild Geese

... I saw a flock of geese flying over the meadows along the rift of dying, golden light, their great wings beating with a slow and solemn beauty, their musical, bell-like cry filling the lonely levels and the dark. Is there a nobler wild clamour in all the world? I listened to the sound till it died away and the birds had disappeared into darkness, and then heard a quiet sea chiding a little at the turn of the tide. ...

—*The Outermost House*

The Last of the Terns

... my last sight of the great summer throng of terns ... was an unforgettable experience. On Saturday, September 3rd ... as I opened the ... door, I found the air above the dunes was snowy with young terns. The day had been mild, and the late afternoon light was mild and rosy golden ... high in space and golden light the myriads of birds drifted and whirled like leaves. North and south we saw them for miles along the dunes. For twenty minutes, perhaps, or half an hour, the swarming filled my sky, and during all that time I did not hear a single bird utter a sound. ... The birds were flying high, higher than I had ever seen terns go. ... It was a rapture, a glory of the young. And this was the last of the terns.

—*The Outermost House*

Yes, the sparrow has found a house, and the swallow a nest for herself, where she may lay her young.

—*Psalms 84*

Dwellings

To every thing there is a season, and a time to every purpose under the heaven.

A time to be born, and a time to die, a time to plant, and a time to pluck up that which is planted. ...

—*Ecclesiastes, Chapter 3:1–8*

All Seasons

The spider taketh hold with her hands, and is in Kings' palaces.

—*Proverbs, 30:28*

The Ubiquitous Spider

It is the glory of God to conceal things, but the glory of kings is to search things out.

—*Old Testament, Proverb, 25:2*

The Way of God and Man

For there is nothing hid, except to be made manifest; nor is anything secret, except to come to light.

—*New Testament, Mark 4:22*

Nature Concealed, Nature Revealed

To him that is joined to all the living there is hope: for a living dog is better than a dead lion.

—*Ecclesiastes, Chapter 9:4*

Invaluable Life

The Fate of Men and Beasts

For the fate of the sons of men and the fate of beasts is the same; as one dies so dies the other. They all have the same breath, and man has no advantage over the beasts; for all is vanity. All go to one place, all are from the dust, and all turn to dust again. Who knows whether the spirit of a man goes upward and the spirit of the beast goes down to the earth? So I saw that there is nothing better than that of a man should enjoy his work, for that is his lot: who can bring him to see what will be after him?

—*Ecclesiastes, Chapter 3:19–22*

BLAKE, WILLIAM (1757–1827)
English poet and artist

To Keep a Joy

He who bends to himself a Joy
Doth the winged life destroy;
But he who kisses the joy as it flies
Lives in Eternity's sunrise

—*Eternity*

A Bird in a Cage

A Robin Redbreast in a cage
Puts all heaven in a rage

—*Proverbs, Line 1*

Logic of Truth

What is now proved was once only imagined, ...
—*The Marriage of Heaven and Hell*

Cruelty to Animals

He who shall hurt the little wren,
Shall never be belov'd by men
—*Auguries of Innocence*

BLANTON, SMILEY (1882–1966)
American author and psychiatrist

A Chinese proverb says: "He who asks a
question is a fool for five minutes; he who does
not ask a question remains a fool forever."
— *Love or Perish*

A Fool Forever

BOLLES, FRANK (1856–1894)
American writer and secretary of Harvard
University (1877)

I have a friend who says that March water is
bluer than any other. It certainly carries its
blueness straighter into the heart. ...
— *At the North of Bearcamp Water*

Blueness of March Water

Not to drink from a New Hampshire brook
is almost as much of a slight as not to bow to a
friend, or not to kiss a little child when she lifts
her face for the good-night caress. ...
— *At the North of Bearcamp Water*

*Not to Drink from a
New Hampshire Brook*

Many is the winter evening ... I have sat by
the fireside and gazed into the red flame of the
blazing "light wood". ... As the pitch grew hot
and burst through the dry wood, whining and
whistling ... its voice and warmth have carried
me back in spirit to the brown beds of fern, the
busy chipmunks under the old oak in the wall,
or to the mayflowers gathered in spring from the
edges of the lingering snow banks.
— *At the North of Bearcamp Water*

Fireside Recollections

Escape from Daily Tasks

No matter how tightly the body may be chained to the wheel of daily duties, the spirit is free ... to bear itself away from noise and vexation into the secret places of the mountains.
—*At the North of Bearcamp Water*

Harvest Moon over a Mountain Lake

When the harvest moon is large and the nights clear, I love to spend an evening hour or two under the great oak-tree on the short of my lonely lake. The soft mists creep across the water, bats flit back and forth squeaking, the whipporwills call to each other that the time for migration is near at hand, and sometimes the voices of the barred owls wake weird echoes in the lake's curves.
—*At the North of Bearcamp Water*

Men Who Live in Cities

Men who live only in great cities may be pitied for being atheists, for they see little beyond the impurity of man; ...
—*At the North of Bearcamp Water*

Night and Day

There is something inexpressibly touching and inspiring in the combination of fading night, with its planets still glowing, and the bird's song of welcome to the day. Night is more eloquent in telling of the wonders of the vast creation. Day tells ... less of peace, more of contest; less of immortality, more of the perishable.
—*At the North of Bearcamp Water*

The Promise of Pines

No one can look at a pine-tree in winter without knowing that spring will come again in due time.
—*At the North of Bearcamp Water*

The heart of the mountain is the wild ravine where these two streams mingle in perpetual coolness and shadow. No path leads to it and few are the feet which have found a way to its beauties. There is a peculiar charm in a spot unknown to the many. Its loneliness endears it to the mind, and gives its associations a rarer flavor.

—*At the North of Bearcamp Water*

The pines below my breezy hilltop tempted me by their music. ... The wind sang in their tops, ... and it took me back to the moment in my earliest childhood when I was first conscious of that soft, soothing music. I do not know when it was, nor where it was, nor how young I may have been, but I can recall ... a sudden feeling of happiness at hearing the voice of the pines. ... If we are in tune with Nature, all her music can find a way into the heart. ...

—*At the North of Bearcamp Water*

Upland woods are cleaner, stronger, more symmetrical than swamp growth, but they have not the effect of tropical luxuriance which the swamp forest possesses.

—*At the North of Bearcamp Water*

Prejudice Against Botany

I recalled one melancholy morning when my teacher, who knew neither the derivation of botanical terms nor the true beauties of botanical science, ordered me to commit to memory the adjectives applied to the various shapes of leaves. The dose prejudiced me against botany for full ten years of my life, yet here in this glistening carpet of the swamp I saw "lanceolate," "auriculate," "cordate," "pinnate," written, not in letters of gold, but in something equally impressive to the memory, and much more easy for a dull teacher to obtain.

—*At the North of Bearcamp Water*

The Sweetest Singer of the Mountains

A long, pure note, followed by one much higher, ... formed the song of my companion on the heights. It was the farewell to the day of a white-throated sparrow, that sweetest singer of the mountain peaks. A feeling of forlornness which had been creeping over me was dispelled. Let the storm come; I was ready for it.

—*At the North of Bearcamp Water*

The Amusing Winter Wren

The winter wren is an amusing little migrant. He seems to have an underground railway of his own from the grim northern forest straight toward a milder clime. Sometimes he appears at an opening in a stone wall and scolds mankind for picking blackberries or plucking goldenrod; again he emerges from the darkness beneath a log in the swamp, and bustles about with the offensive energy of a special policeman.

—*At the North of Bearcamp Water*

These chickadees, alert, courageous, tireless and generous, are the convoys of the warbler fleets. ... Then, far away, will be heard the faint "*dee-dee*" of the titmouse. ... presently a dozen or twen-ty little birds are seen hovering, darting, flitting, but steadily advancing tree by tree, through the woods. Perhaps not more than one in ten will be a chickadee, yet it is the chicka-dee which gives character and direction to the body.

—*At the North of Bearcamp Water*

Chickadee Convoys

A field of buckwheat or other small grain is a magnet in the days when the birds are wander-ing. To it come the song sparrows, chipping sparrows, white-throats, juncos, purple finches, field sparrows, goldfinches, and bay-winged buntings. They love to linger many days in the stubble; and when bird music is rare, their occasional songs are precious to the ear. ...

—*At the North of Bearcamp Water*

Buckwheat Fields and Birds

Sparrows love fences, stone walls and their accompanying growths of berry-bushes and small trees. ... our New England substitutes for the hedge-rows of the Old World, ...

—*At the North of Bearcamp Water*

Sparrows, Fences, and Stone Walls

Many of the birds go south cheerfully, or indifferently, but the bluebirds seem to linger sadly and lovingly, and to feel that the migra-tion is an enforced exile from the home they love best.

—*At the North of Bearcamp Water*

Bluebirds and Migration

The End of Migration

As the early October days glide by, waves of migration come faster and faster, their acceleration seeming, ... like the ever quicker throbbing of the air under the wing-beats of the grouse. Even as the drumming suddenly ceases and the summer air seems still and heavy in the silence which follows, so the migration suddenly ends, and the woods and fields become very still in the late Indian summer.

—*At the North of Bearcamp Water*

Hawk Flight

All through the month of September hawks abound. They circle around the peak of Chocorua, seemingly for the pleasure of it. ... Sometimes great flocks of hawks pass across the sky, not circling, as the red-tailed and red-shouldered hawks are so fond of doing, but sailing straight before the wind like a fleet of mackerelmen running down the coast wing and wing. ... The stately progress of these birds, moving many miles an hour without a wing-beat ... is one of the wonders of nature.

—*At the North of Bearcamp Water*

BORLAND, HAL (1900–1978)
American naturalist, author, philosopher and novelist; winner of the John Burroughs Medal for *Hill Country Harvest* (1968)

Beginnings

The world is full of beginnings now, and beginnings are often more interesting, sometimes even more important, than what follows. The vernal change has started.

But the great change comes now before the full flowering. Now is the deep wonder, for the bud itself is the miracle. To watch the upthrust of a daffodil, to see it take form as a flower-to-be, to see the bud grow and take on the warmth of color—there is the very synthesis of spring. But once open, it is a flower, color, perfected beauty; and once open it begins to fade, imperceptibly but also inevitably.

Thus it is with a bud, all buds. Spring is there in the flower within the bud, but the miracle is in the beginning, the way that bud opens. You see a birch on the hillside, its buds fat against the sky. You watch the ... tips appear, when the tree stands in all the delicacy of April's green mist, ... Or the way bloodroom comes to flower, opening that fat green bud. Or the way a violet lifts its buds for the sunlight to warm and slowly unfold. That, to me, is April, the swelling bud, the beginning.

Today I went up and saw April among the birches.

—Book of Days

July 6

It was not a peaceful age, that Age of Reptiles. Last summer I saw a primitive battle that, in a very minor way, reflected some of the violence of that ancient time.

It was a struggle to the death between a big snapping turtle and a five-foot water snake, and it was fought in a marshy flat at the mouth of one of the nearby brooks. How the snapper got a hold on the snake in the first place I do not know, but when I first saw them the snake was caught in those wire-cutter jaws, only the front two thirds of its body free.

It was a hopeless fight. The snake had no weapons but its constricting coils and the battering but fangless blows it could deal with its head. The snapper was not only armed, mouth and claw, but it was armored with its heavy shell. The snake hammered at the snapper's head and neck, striking repeatedly with no effect. It threw a coil of its body around the snapper's shell, tightened till its muscles corded, and the snapper merely braced its feet. With a twist, the snake flipped the turtle onto its back. The turtle's hind feet reached and raked with vicious claws and the snake's hold loosened. The turtle scrambled to its feet again.

Half a dozen times the snake looped and squeezed, with no effect at all. The turtle kept shifting its hold, each new bite taking more of the snake's vitality. Finally the snake swung a body coil toward the turtle's neck, its one chance of victory. Had it been able to catch the neck, the battle would have been over, probably a Pyrrhic victory, for the snake was crucially hurt. But it failed. The turtle, snapping with amazing speed, caught the snake just behind the head. That settled it, though the snake flipped the turtle over twice more in its desperate thrashing. At last it began to relax, the relaxation of defeat and death.

While I watched, there in the reedy marsh, I knew I was seeing, in modern miniature, even to the setting, the kind of battle to death that must have occurred constantly 100 million years ago. And such battles were always fought between reptiles, because there were no other major combatants on the land anywhere.

—*Book of Days*

July 14

The blacksnake on my mountain and the turtle in my river do not speak of language I can understand. They have nowhere near the brain capacity I have. I cannot grant them much intelligence, nor any imagination, love or compassion. I am sure their powers of memory are limited. But they are here today, and their presence proves that the reptile, for all its cold blood, its oviparous birth, and its limited brain power, is a persistent and successful form of life. In its own way, that life has adapted to far more change than man has ever known. I can only hope that my own kind has as much persistence, as a species, as these reptilian neighbors of mine.

—*Book of Days*

The Successful Reptiles

Plant Survival

A Walk in the Midst of Infinity

July 22

There are no idealists in the plant world, and there is no compassion. The rose and the morning glory know no mercy. Bindweed, the wild morning glory, will quietly choke its competitors to death, and the fencerow rose will just as quietly crowd out any other plant that tried to share its roothold. Idealism and mercy are human terms and human concepts. Nature doesn't seem to be concerned with them.

—*Book of Days*

December 26

We have gone for a walk, up the road, not across the snow-covered pastures, almost every evening the past week. The moon has passed its full, now rises late, but the stars are magnificent. They seem to have the deep fireglow of eternity. … to walk abroad now is to walk in the midst of infinity. There are no limits to either time of distance, except as man himself may make them. I have only to touch the wind to know these things, for the wind itself is full of starlight, even as the frozen earth underfoot, starlight and endless time and exalted wonder.

I look at the red-gold star we call Arcturus, and even as the ancients I strain for a closer look, through this peephole, this spark-burn in the blanket of night, hoping for the slightest glimpse of Beyond. I turn to the star called Betelgeuse, even redder than Arcturus, and I have to accept the factual truth of the astronomers, and yet wonder if that is all, the whole, the ultimate truth.

Time and distance, and wonder—we walk up this valley in the midst of eternity.

—*Book of Days*

December 31

Year-end, now. And year's-beginnings, and an old custom to face realities when the totting-up has been done.

The headlines in the morning's news are not encouraging. Man still cannot be trusted to save himself from his own folly. The greatness and the glory seems all to be in the past. Perhaps it was always thus—greatness and glory are hard to recognize in the glare of today, any today. And yet there is that about which to dream as well as the lure of visions. And forever there is change, the one constant. Change.

Here we are, in the homeland. It is winter, and it will be spring again. We have known other winters, and survived them.

We have known this year, intimately. We have set down the questions and sought the answers and set them down. And here we are now, at year's end, watching the weather, accepting it, knowing all things change, knowing spring follows winter.

I can report now that grass grows, flowers bloom, birds sing. I can report that the sun rises and sets, the moon keeps its own schedule, the stars follow patterns they have followed since man first saw them in the night sky. I know these truths. Lesser truths will take more learning, but I can live with what I now know.

—*Book of Days*

The Constancy of Change

BROWNE, SIR THOMAS (1605–1682)
English writer, scholar, physician, scientist and philosopher

The Divinity of Man

There is surely a piece of divinity in us; something that was before the elements and owes no homage to the sun.

—*Religio Medici in*
Literary Masters of England

BROWNING, ROBERT (1812–1889)
English poet

Reaching

Ah, but a man's reach should exceed his grasp,
Or what's a heaven for?

—*Andrea del Sarto*

BURGESS, ANTHONY (1917–   )
English author, columnist, composer, play producer, lecturer and teacher

To Try to Be Nicer

All the great novels have been about people trying to be kinder, more tolerant. Aldous Huxley concluded at the end of his hard-thinking life that all you could ask of people was that they try to be a little nicer.

—*"Modern Novels: The 99 Best"*
The New York Times,
Sunday, February 5, 1984

BURNFORD, SHEILA (1918–1984)

Writer and novelist; awarded medal by Canadian Book Club of the Year for *Children* (1963) and Lewis Carroll Shelf Award for *The Incredible Journey* (1971)

I was very glad to see this particular [dog] team returned, to be staked out on the grass above the rocky embankment just below for it contained Marmalade, my baritone lead. Shortly afterward I was able to record him against the most wonderful background sounds on the ice, red-throated loons, about eight of them. Their high haunting crying started with a rhythmic beat and merged into another part where they sounded as though they were *almost* going to continue into the lovely call of the common loon, but ended there tantalizingly instead.

My baritone was very large, one of the biggest dogs around, with marmalade-fringed ears, and two large round spots immediately above his eyes, which made him look as though he had four eyes. He sang like a virtuoso, with his whole soul, his lower jaw trembling on a particularly long, drawn-out musical howl. His teammates, all sitting with their eyes on him as though he were the conductor, waited until he finished, then one by one took up the chorus.

—*One Woman's Arctic*

Songs of the Arctic

Tragedy of an Aged Husky

... When it saw me at the tent flap, the dog hesitated, then halted, about a hundred yards away He was still in his thickest winter coat; but through the glasses I saw that the coat was shabby and worn down to the skin in places, and that he was old.

Then to my horror, he wagged his tail. I wish he hadn't. I wish he had looked at me with all the cold indifference that Eskimo dogs show toward a stranger. But this one was so desperate to placate any human being that he wagged his tail.

One of the men erupted from the hut, fired a shot and yelled "Scram you ... old bag of bones." ... I knew what was going to happen and knew it was the only thing to do and the most merciful, because there was no longer any place for this dog in the order of things; this was the Arctic, not suburbia. ... Yet this husky, who had wagged his tail so uneasily before us just now was a dog who had lived and worked in the cruelest possible elements for his entire life, straining his heart out in harness, goaded on by the whip or staked out to a short chain in the non-working months, to fight and pant with thirst with his team, his only reward the hunk of seal or fish flung down once or twice a week, his only anticipation that of running in the traces again. In spite of all this, he had sought out man again ... and shown by the only means in his power that he was ready to do the whole thing over again.

But we had no use for him. At another threat, he dragged himself back a few yards, then, when once again there was no movement outside the hut, he regained the ground. John came out with a rifle, and lay down to take aim. The dog wagged his tail again, there was a crack, and he fell. There was no movement, only the stiff, injured hind leg lowering slowly down to the heather. He had known nothing; he was all right now.

But I was not all right, not at peace. I had known something. And what I knew I did not like or understand; the whole human race of which I was a part.

—*One Woman's Arctic*

BURROUGHS, JOHN (1837–1921)
American naturalist, author, poet and essayist

March 1, 1899

Unless you can write about Nature with feeling, with real love, with more or less hearty affiliation and comradeship with her, it is no use. Your words will not stick. They will awaken no response in the reader. There are two or three writers now making books upon outdoor themes that I find I cannot read. The page has no savor; it is dry and tasteless. The writers have taken up these nature themes deliberately, as they might any other; they have no special call to write upon them. I have tried hard to be interested in Gibson's work, but I cannot. It lacks juice, unction. There is feeling in his drawings but not in his text. Bradford Torrey is the only nature writer at the present time whose work I can read.

—*The Heart of Burroughs Journals*

What Nature Writing Requires—Tribute to Bradford Torrey

To Walk Alone

Every lover of Nature understands Thoreau's aversion to a companion in a walk, except he be a true lover also. It is a rare qualification to be a good walker. We do not go to the woods for society, or to talk politics; and he that would go with me, must leave me to myself, and leave the town behind him. A young and thoughtful boy is the best company. You do not want to be diverted or hindered, but open, like a sponge, yet ready to give or take.

—*The Heart of Burroughs Journals*

A Prescription for Happiness

I have discovered the secret of happiness— it is work, either with the hands or the head— something to do. It is the only safe and sure ground of happiness. The moment I have something to do, the draughts are open and my chimney draws, and I am happy. The trouble is generally that we do not know when we are happy.

—*The Heart of Burroughs Journals*

Sex—A Consummation of Love

There is no greater or more significant fact in the universe than that of sex; none with larger and deeper running analogies; nothing like the love of the man for the woman, and the responding love of the woman, nothing so ravishing and fearfully uncontrollable as the sexual desire, nothing so sacred and beautiful as the consummation of love; and no instincts more certain and constant than those which throw the veil over these things. And this tragedy of love must be rendered, if at all, with perfect fidelity to Nature and the natural instincts and promptings.

—*The Heart of Burroughs Journals*

Let me work all day in my garden, the next day ramble in the fields and woods, with a little reading, and the third day I can give myself to literary pursuits with a new freshness and vigor.
—*The Heart of Burroughs Journals*

Warm-up for Writing

Winter drives a man back upon himself, and tests his powers of self-entertainment.
—*Introduction to Wake-Robin*

Test of Winter

… the phoebe-bird, builds an exquisite nest of moss on the side of some shelving cliff or over-hanging rock. The other day … my eyes rested upon one of these structures, looking precisely as if it grew there, so in keeping was it with the mossy character of the rock, and I have had a growing affection for the bird ever since. The rock seemed to love the nest and to claim it as its own. I said, What a lesson in architecture is here!
—*Wake-Robin*

A Lesson in Architecture

Take the first step in ornithology, … and you are ticketed for the whole voyage. There is a fascination about it quite overpowering. It fits so well with other things—with fishing, hunting, farming, walking, camping, with all that takes one to the fields and woods. Secrets lurk on all sides. There is news in every bush. What no man ever saw before may the next moment be revealed to you. What a new interest the woods have! How you long to explore every nook and corner of them! … the student of ornithology has an advantage over his companions. He has one more resource, one more avenue of delight. His game is everywhere.
—*Wake-Robin*

The Invitation

The Lure of Primitive Woods

In visiting vast, primitive, far-off woods, one naturally expects to find something rare and precious, or something entirely new. ... Thoreau made three excursions into the Maine woods, and, though he started the moose and caribou, had nothing more novel to report by way of bird notes, than the songs of the wood–thrush and the pewee. This was my own experience in the Adirondacs.

—*Wake-Robin*

Book—The Guide

Ornithology cannot be learned satisfactorily from the books. The satisfaction is in learning it from nature. One must have an original experience with the birds. The books are only the guide, the invitation.

—*Wake-Robin*

The Most Precious Things

Bought knowledge is dear at any price. The most precious things have no commercial value.

—*Wake-Robin*

The Blooming of Flowers, The Arrival of Birds

The dandelion tells me when to look for the swallow, the dog–toothed violet when to expect the wood-thrush, and when I have found the wake-robin in bloom I know the season is fairly begun.

—*Wake-Robin*

Interpreting Nature

To interpret Nature is not to improve upon her; it is to draw her out; it is to have an emotional intercourse with her, absorb her and reproduce her tinged with the colors of the spirit.

—*Wake-Robin*

When Nature made the bluebird she wished to propitiate both the sky and the earth, so she gave him the color of the one on his back and the hue of the other on his breast, and ordained that his appearance in spring should denote that the strife and war between these two elements was at an end. He is the peace-harbinger. ... He means the furrow and he means the warmth; he means all the soft, wooing influences of the spring ... the retreating footsteps of winter.

—*Wake-Robin*

The Bluebird

There is ever a lurking suspicion that the beginning of things is in some way associated with water, and one may notice that in his private walks he is led by a curious attraction to fetch all the springs and ponds in his route, as if by them was the place for wonders and miracles to happen.

—*Wake-Robin*

Wonders and Miracles in Waterways

In that free, fascinating, half-work and half-play pursuit, sugar-making, ... the robin is one's constant companion. When the day is sunny and the ground bare, you meet him at all points and hear him at all hours. At sunset, on the tops of the tall maples, with look heavenward, and in a spirit of utter abandonment, he carols his simple strain. And sitting thus amid the stark, silent trees, above the wet, cold earth, with the chill of winter still in the air, there is no fitter or sweeter songster in the whole round year.

—*Wake-Robin*

Robins and Sugar-Making

All Birds Are Songsters

All birds are incipient or would-be songsters in the spring. I find corroborative evidence of this even in the crowing of the cock. The flowering of the maple is not so obvious as that of the magnolia; nevertheless, there is inflorescence.

—*Wake-Robin*

The Bird Parasite

It is a singular freak of Nature, this instinct which prompts one bird to lay its eggs in the nest of others, and thus shirk the responsibility of rearing its own young. The cow buntings always resort to this cunning trick. ... The other day, in a tall tree in the woods, I discovered the black-throated green-backed warbler devoting itself to this dusky, overgrown foundling. An old farmer to whom I pointed out the fact was much surprised that such things should happen in his woods, without his knowledge.

—*Wake-Robin*

The Profit of Bird Study in June

June, of all the months, the student of ornithology can least afford to lose. Most birds are nesting then, and in full song and plumage.

—*Wake-Robin*

A Bird and Its Voice

It seems to me that I do not know a bird until I have heard its voice; ... A bird's song contains a clue to its life, and establishes a sympathy, an understanding, between itself and the listener.

—*Wake-Robin*

Our Best Songsters

If we take the quality of melody as the test, the wood-thrush, hermit-thrush, and the veery-thrush stand at the head of our list of songsters.

—*Wake-Robin*

... the song of the hermit thrush ... suggests a serene religious beatitude as no other sound in nature ... it is perhaps more of an evening than a morning hymn. ... "O spheral, spheral!" he seems to say; "O holy, holy! O clear away, clear away! O clear up, clear up!" interspersed with the finest trills and the most delicate preludes. It is not a proud, gorgeous strain like the tanager's or the grossbeak's; suggests no passion or emotion—nothing personal—but seems to be the voice of that calm, sweet solemnity one attains in his best moments.

—*Wake-Robin*

Song of the Hermit Thrush

The soft, mellow flute of the veery fills a place in the chorus of the woods that the song of the vesper–sparrow fills in the chorus of the fields. It has the nightingale's habit of singing in the twilight, as have all our thrushes. Walk out toward the forest in the warm twilight of a June day, and when fifty rods distant you will hear their soft, reverberating notes, rising from a dozen different throats.

—*Wake-Robin*

Song of the Veery

Who has seen the partridge drum? It is the next thing to catching a weasel asleep, though by much caution and tact it may be done.

—*Wake-Robin*

The Drumming of the Partridge

The woods hold not such another gem as the nest of the humming-bird. The finding of one is an event to date from. ... I have met with but two, both by chance.

—*Wake-Robin*

The Nest of the Hummingbird

Seeing the Finer, Inner World of Nature

The powers of observation of country people are not fine enough and trained enough. They see and hear coarsely. An object must be big and a sound loud, to attract their attention. Have you seen and heard the kinglet? If not, the finer inner world of nature is a sealed book to you. When your senses take in a kinglet, they will take in a thousand other objects that now escape you.

—*In Warbler Time*

To Know Joy in the Living Bird

To the real nature-lover the bird in the bush is worth much more than the bird in the hand, because the nature-lover is not after a specimen; he is after a living fact; he is after a new joy in life.

It is an important part, but by no means the main part of what ornithology holds for us, to be able to name every bird on sight or call. To love the bird, to appreciate its place in the landscape and in the season, to relate it to your daily life, to divine its character, to know it emotionally in your heart—that is much more. To know the birds as the sportsman knows his game; to experience the same thrill purged of all thoughts of slaughter: to make their songs music in your life—this is indeed something to be desired.

—*John Burroughs, Introduction to* Bird Neighbors *by Neltje Blanchan*

FOURTH EARL OF CHESTERFIELD (1694–1773)
(PHILLIP DORMER STANHOPE)
    Statesman and man of letters

    It is only the manner of saying or writing it that makes it appear new. Convince yourself that manner is almost everything, in everything; and study it accordingly.

        —Lord Chesterfield's
            Letters to His Son

Manner Is Everything

CHRISTENSEN, CLYDE M. (1905–)
    Educator, author and professor of plant pathology

    To many this prying into the secrets of the minor marvels of nature appears futile, a business of learning more and more about less and less, but this yearning to find out what makes nature work, and why and how, is the basis of all research. If we are eventually to control nature, we must know something about how nature operates. An intelligent and thorough study of the most humble dung fungus will add something to our accumulated body of knowledge, our understanding, our culture, even as does the study of minor stars whose light started off to us a couple of hundred million light years ago, or the forces in the atom, or what makes music. Sometimes the facts are of value in themselves, … now and then someone finds a key that opens a whole new field.

        —The Molds and Man

*Learning About the
Minor Marvels of Nature*

Fundamental Research and Mycology

Fundamental research, which has as its aim only the discovery of more and more of nature's secrets, seems necessary to provide the environment—the backlog of information and ideas—that spawns usable discoveries. "God bless higher mathematics," as a mathematics professor is reported to have said, "and may they never be of any use to anybody." One may say the same of mycology.

—*The Molds and Man*

Scientific Snobbery— Still with Us

Shortly after 1800 a Danish school teacher proved that rust from barberry leaves could be transmitted to rye plants. Nobody paid much attention to his work, partly because it was not widely publicized, partly because he was only a high school teacher, and not a "scientist." He had not paid his dues to the scientific fraternity; he did not have the handshake—a form of snobbery that is by no means a thing of the past.

—*The Molds and Man*

An Occupational Disease

… professors, after long years of teaching, are apt to confuse their lecture notes with the fountain of truth. It is an occupational disease.

—*The Molds and Man*

CHURCHILL, SIR WINSTON (1874–1965)
(LEONARD SPENCER)

English statesman, author, Prime Minister of
England, famed speaker and winner of the
Nobel Prize for literature (1953)

Quotations when engraved upon the
memory give you good thoughts. They also
make you anxious to read the author and to look
for more.

—*Nature Interlude*

COLERIDGE, SAMUEL TAYLOR (1772–1834)
English poet and critic

Why are not more gems from our great
authors scattered over the country? Great books
are not in everybody's reach; and though it is
better to know them thoroughly than to know
them only here and there, yet it is a good work
to give a little to those who have neither the
time nor means to get more. Let every book-
worm, when ... he discovers a sentence, a story,
an illustration, that does his heart good, hasten
to give it. ...

*Gems from
Our Great Authors*

On the Use of Time

COMAN, DALE REX (1906–)

Pathologist, educator, author and professor of plant pathology

Time is precious stuff. But it is not worth a damn unless you are profligate of it. Time is not a commodity to be saved and hoarded like stock certificates in a safety vault or cash in a bank, nor is its expenditure to be regarded as a deduction from one's budget. Time should never be ticked off as a spent portion on calendar or clock; it should never be saved, for it accrues no interest.

I prize time above all other possessions and spend it like water, having learned long ago that its purchasing power far exceeds that of dollar bills. With time I can buy such priceless items as peace and happiness, which I do not see listed on the stock exchange. I can buy a chunk of utter idleness, the glorious idleness to which I have every intention of devoting this day.

The abandonment of purposeful activity does not necessarily mean doing nothing. It may entail doing but with no designated objective or destination. It means drifting wherever you happen to drift. You cannot plan a dissipative day; it must be allowed to unfold as you proceed, without effort or schedule, and you must allow yourself to be carried along with it, not propel your way through it.

—*The Endless Adventure*

Never Hasten the Day

One must never be in haste to end a day; there are too few of them in a lifetime.

—*The Endless Adventure*

The charm of a woodland road lies not only in its beauty but in anticipation. Around each bend may be a discovery, an adventure. A familiar road is like an old friend who every so often startles with an unexpected quirk of personality, while a heretofore untraveled one is a new acquaintance whose character is yet to be appraised.

—*The Endless Adventure*

CONFUCIUS (551–497 B.C.)
Chinese political and ethical philosopher and teacher.

If the search for riches were sure to be successful, though I should become a groom with whip in hand to get them, I will do so. As the search may not be successful, I will follow after that which I love.

The Charm of a Woodland Road

Choices

COTT, HUGH B. (1900–1987)
Lecturer in zoology and Strickland curator,
University of Cambridge, England

*The Struggle
for Existence*

One of the fundamental facts affecting
living creatures is the interspecific warfare
known to biology as the struggle for existence.
Animals, like men, are beset by many and great
dangers. The problem of self-preservation in the
field is very real, very urgent, and often difficult
enough to solve; but it is one with which all
forms of animal life are faced. Broadly speaking,
individual survival depends upon the satisfaction of two vital needs—security and suste-
nance. These are the two primary claims of life.
In a world peopled with potential enemies and
pregnant with hunger and the possibility of
starvation, if an animal is to survive, it must eat,
and avoid being eaten. It is the old question of
the relation between the aggressor and the
victim of aggression, between the hunter and
the hunted.
  —*Preface to "Adaptive Coloration in Animals"*

COUES, ELLIOTT (1842–1890)
American ornithologist, scientist, naturalist,
speaker and writer

*To Reason—
The Beginning of Science*

The history of American ornithology begins
at the time when men first wrote upon American birds; for men write nothing without some
reason, and to reason at all is the beginning of
science, even as to reason aright is its end.
  —*Key to North American Birds*

For myself, the time is past, happily or not, when every bird was an agreeable surprise, for dewdrops do not last all day; but I have never yet walked in the woods without learning something pleasant that I did not know before. I should consider a bird new to science ample reward for a month of steady work; one bird new to a locality would repay a week's search; a day is happily spent that shows me any bird that I never saw alive before. How then can you with so much before you, keep out of the woods another minute?

—*Key to North American Birds*

The Harvest of the Bird Hunter

COWPER, WILLIAM (1731–1800)
English pre-romantic poet

I would not enter on my list of friends
(Though graced with polished manners
    and fine sense,
Yet wanting sensibility), the man
Who needlessly sets foot upon a worm.
    —*The Task, Book VI, Winter Walk at Noon*

Needless Acts

God made the country and man made the town.
    —*The Task*

Boulders and Bricks

How Some Seeds Get About

DARWIN, CHARLES ROBERT (1809–1882)
English naturalist and original expounder of the theory of evolution ("Darwinism")

I do not believe that botanists are aware how charged the mud of ponds is with seeds; I have tried several little experiments, but will here give only the most striking cases: I took in February three tablespoonfuls of mud from three different points, beneath water, on the edge of a little pond: this mud when dried weighed only 6 3/4 ounces; I kept it covered up in my study for six months, pulling up and counting each plant as it grew; the plants were of many kinds, and were altogether 537 in number: and yet the viscid mud was all contained in a breakfast cup! Considering these facts, I think it would be an inex-plicable circumstance if water-birds did not transport the seeds of fresh-water plants to unstocked ponds and streams, situated at very distant points. ... Even small fish swallow seeds of moderate size, as of the yellow water-lily and Potamogeton. Herons and other birds, century after century, have gone on daily devouring fish; they then take flight and go to other waters, or are blown across the sea; and we have seen that seeds retain their power of germination, when rejected many hours afterwards in pellets or in the excrement.

—*The Origin of Species*

DAVIS, HENRY E. (1859–1890)

Lawyer, South Carolina naturalist and sportsman and authority on the wild turkey

To Master a Swamp

You will never completely master a river swamp, or any other wooded area, unless you repeatedly traverse it, and you can not do this until you know how the land lies, what are the prominent landmarks, and what are the feasible routes to follow in exploring it.

—*The American Wild Turkey*

DAVIS, WILLIAM T. (1862–1945)

American businessman, naturalist and amateur entomologist

An Advantage of Fresh Fields

One of the chief advantages in visiting different meadows and pieces of woodland is that it whets our perception; we are more on the look out. ... Probably there isn't a ten-acre woodlot, even near home, that has been thoroughly explored. If you think there is, go through it again, and see if there isn't a nut tree that you have ... passed by without discovery.

—*Days Afield on Staten Island*

Man and Artificial Things

A man who concerns himself principally with the artificial, and who thinks that the world is for ... business alone, misses entirely the divine halo that rests about much in nature. ... We must not put by entirely the chippy singing in the apple tree, or the white clouds, for nature declares a dividend every hour.

—*Days Afield on Staten Island*

Nature Is No Jester

There is no jesting in nature; she may seem glad or sad, but she is earnest. A trifling man in the field cannot fool the crickets.

—*Days Afield on Staten Island*

The Gentle Bluebird

When a bluebird calls to its mate from a telegraph wire it bears truly a message of love. His voice is mild and is in sympathy with the more kindly human messages that are carried unknown to him by the wire beneath his feet. He seems to have been born a gentleman, to be incapable of any meanness, and he has much of "that inbread loyalty unto virtue."

—*Days Afield on Staten Island*

DAY, CLARENCE SHEPARD, JR. (1874–1935)
American humorous writer and son of the famous lawyer, Clarence Day

The People and Nature

They [the people] will think of Nature as "something to go out and look at." They will try to live wholly apart from her and forget they're her sons. Forget? They will even deny it, and declare themselves sons of God. In spite of her wonders they will regard Nature as somehow too humble to be the true parent of such prominent people as simians. They will lose all respect for the dignity of fair Mother Earth, and whisper to each other she is an evil and indecent old person. They will snatch at her gifts, pry irreverently into her mysteries, and ignore half the warnings they get from her about how to live.

—*This Simian World*

DE LA MARE, WALTER (1873–1956)
English poet, novelist, anthologist and romantic writer

... bright towers of silence ...
—"England"

Clouds

DE MORGAN, AUGUSTUS (1806–1871)
English writer

Great fleas have little fleas upon their
    backs to bite 'em,
And little fleas have lesser fleas, and so
    ad infinitum.
And the great fleas themselves, in turn,
    have greater fleas to go on;
While these again have greater still, and
    greater still, and so on.
—*A Budget of Paradoxes*

Flea Circus

DEVOE, ALAN (1909–1955)
American naturalist and author

In all the universe around us, and in the secret regions of our own secret hearts, instinct everywhere pervades: profound unlearned impulsions giving guidance to the lives of ants and birds and beasts and men and all the creatures of the earth.
—*Lives Around Us*

Instinct Is Everywhere

The Permanence of Nature

Frogs will be croaking and mating and feeding when today's hot warriors have been dust for many a millenium. It is good for a man to shift his attention for a while to something as permanent as a frog.

—*Lives Around Us*

Blood on the Wind

The quietest woodland, the serenest meadow drowsing under the sun, is hourly the scene of uncountable carnages. To have life is to have hunger; to sustain life is to require the sacrifice of other lives. In the natural world there is always the smell of newly spilled blood on the wind— ...

—*Lives Around Us*

Instinct Is Unaltering

The sense of instinct is not flexible, like thought. It is rigid and unaltering, like the succession of the seasons.

—*Lives Around Us*

Role of the Weasel

For every creature under the sun there is a particular role in the natural scheme: for bees the bearing of pollen for the fertilization of plants and trees, for earthworms the aerating of the soil to make it fecund, for a crab or crawfish the scavenging of under-water earth. It is the grim and singular role of a weasel to kill— ... to keep the mice from becoming too many and the cottontails from too far exceeding their number, ...

—*Lives Around Us*

DICKINSON, EMILY (1830–1886)

American poet

To make a prairie it takes a clover and one bee,
One clover, and a bee,
And revery.
The revery alone will do,
If bees are few.

> *—Poem Numbered 1755*
> *—The Complete Poems of Emily Dickinson*

DILLARD, ANNIE (1945–   )

Writer, teacher of poetry and creative writing and distinguished visiting professor at Wesleyan University (1979–1981); winner of the Pulitzer Prize for general nonfiction for *Pilgrim at Tinker Creek* (1975)

There are seven or eight categories of phenomena in the world that are worth talking about, and one of them is the weather. Any time you care to get in your car and drive across the country and over the mountains, come into our valley, cross Tinker Creek, drive up the road to the house, walk across the yard, knock on the door and ask to come in and talk about the weather, you'd be welcome.

> *—Pilgrim at Tinker Creek*

To Catch Spring

I have been thinking about the change of seasons. I don't want to miss spring this year. I want to be there on the spot the moment the grass turns green. I always miss this radical revolution; I see it the next day from a window, the yard so suddenly green and lush I could envy Nebuchadnezzar down on all fours eating grass. This year I want to stick a net into time and say "now." ... But it occurred to me that I could no more catch spring by the tip of the tail than I could untie the apparent knot in the snakeskin; there are no edges to grasp.

—*Pilgrim at Tinker Creek*

The "Input Systems" of Children

When we lose our innocence—when we start feeling the weight of the atmosphere and learn that there's death in the pot—we take leave of our senses. Only children can hear the song of the male house mouse. Only children keep their eyes open. The only thing they *have* got is sense; they have highly developed "input systems," admitting all data indiscriminately. Matt Spireng has collected thousands of arrow-heads and spearheads; he says that if you really want to find arrowheads, you must walk with a child—a child will pick up *everything*. All my adult life I have wished to see the cemented case of a caddisfly larva. It took Sally Moore, the young daughter of friends, to find one on the pebbled bottom of a shallow stream on whose bank we sat side by side. "What's that?" she asked. That, I wanted to say as I recognized the prize she held, is a memento mori for people who read too much.

—*Pilgrim at Tinker Creek*

Our excessive emotions are so patently painful and harmful to us as a species that I can hardly believe that they evolved. Other creatures manage to have effective matings and even stable societies without great emotions, and they have a bonus in that they need not ever mourn. (But some higher animals have emotions that we think are similar to ours: dogs, elephants, otters, and the sea mammals mourn their dead. Why do that to an otter? What creator could be so cruel, not to kill others, but to let them care?) It would seem that emotions are the curse, not death—emotions that appear to have devolved upon a few freaks as a special curse from Malevolence.

—*Pilgrim at Tinker Creek*

I heard a clamor in the underbrush beside me, a rustle of an animal's approach. It sounded as though the animal was about the size of a bobcat, a small bear, or a large snake. The commotion stopped and started, coming ever nearer. The agent of all this ruckus proved to be of course a towhee.

The more I see of these bright birds —with black backs, white tail bars, and rufous patches on either side of their white breasts—the more I like them. They are not even faintly shy. They are everywhere, in treetops and on the ground. Their song reminds me of a child's neighborhood rallying cry—ee-ock-ee—with a heart-felt warble at the end. But it is their call that is especially endearing. The towhee has the brass and grace to call, simply and clearly, "tweet." I know of no other bird that stoops to literal tweeting.

—*Pilgrim at Tinker Creek*

The Endearing, Noisy Towhee

The Great Hurrah

The great hurrah about wild animals is that they exist at all, and the greater hurrah is the actual moment of seeing them. Because they have a nice dignity, and prefer to have nothing to do with me, not even as the simple objects of my vision. They show me by their very wariness what a prize it is simply to open my eyes and behold.

—Pilgrim at Tinker Creek

The Secret Life of Books

What I sought in books was imagination. It was depth, depth of thought and feeling; some sort of extreme of subject matter; some nearness to death; some call to courage. I myself was getting wild; I wanted wildness, originality, genius, rapture, hope. I wanted strength, not tea parties. What I sought in books was a world whose surfaces, whose people and events and days lived, actually matched the exaltation of the interior life. There you could live.

Those of us who read carried around with us like martyrs a secret knowledge, a secret joy, and secret hope: There is a life worth living where history is taking place; there are ideas worth dying for, and circumstances where courage is still prized. This life could be found and joined, like the Resistance. I kept this exhilarating faith alive in myself, concealed under my uniform shirt like an oblate's ribbon; I would not be parted from it.

—An American Childhood

DIMNET, ERNEST (1866–1954)

French abbé, literary critic, traveller, essayist
and biographer; author of *The Bronte Sisters, The
Tendencies of French Thought* and other books

Anybody familiar with country people, even
of the most uncultivated sort, realises that they
appreciate natural beauty, a landscape, the last
smile of autumn on a wood, a sunset, the flash of
a wild bird, quite as much as a professional artist
or versifier. All they lack is words or oftener
confidence; many of them are as loath to speak
of their innermost loves as to change their
accent. ...

—*The Art of Thinking*

*Country People
and Nature*

All children under nine or ten years of age are poets and philosophers. They pretend to live with the rest of us, and the rest of us imagine that we influence them so that their lives are only a reflection of our own. But, as a matter of fact they are as self-contained as cats and as continuously attentive to the magical charm of what they see inwardly. Their mental wealth is extraordinary; only the greatest artists or poets, whose resemblance to children is a banal certainty, can give us some idea of it. A golden-haired little fellow playing with his blocks in the garden may be conscious all the time of the sunset while pretending not to look at it. "Come along!" the nurse said to Felicite de la Mennais, eight years old, "you have looked long enough at those waves and everybody is going away." The answer: "They watch what I am watching, but they do not see what I see," was no brag but merely a plea to stay on. Who can tell what the four Bronte tots saw or did not see in the moors through which, day after day, they rambled holding hands? Most intelligent children ... have the philosopher's doubts about the existence of the world. You see them looking curiously at a stone; you think "children are so funny" and all the time they are wondering if the stone may not be eternal. ... Have I not heard a little girl of nine interrupt a conversation of professors who were talking about nothing to ask the astounding question: "Father, what is beauty? What makes it?"

—*The Art of Thinking*

DOBIE, J. FRANK (1888–1964)
American teacher, historian and folklorist of the Southwest

There are many pleasing sounds in nature. The song of the canyon wren, tripping down, down, down the scale, fills one with lightsomeness. The rising howl of the coyote is not lovely ... but many a time the wild and dark and elemental beauty of it has taken me far away and filled me with a sense of the mysteries.
—*The Voice of the Coyote*

Pleasing Sounds

The instinct of animals, both predators and preyed upon, for waiting in vegetative blankness is beyond the patience of all but a few human beings. The spider at its web and the fawn motionless all day long in its grassy bed, except when its mother comes to suckle it swiftly, are characteristic of the whole animal world. On tireless wings, sweeping the ground of whole townships with telescopic eyes the buzzard "awaits the will of God" with no more apparent restiveness than the bud awaits sap and sunshine to unfold into leaf.
—*The Voice of the Coyote*

Watchful Waiting

Sympathy for wild animals, sympathy that is intellectual as much as emotional, has not been a strong element in the traditional American way of life. ... Among the wise, this civilized sympathy infuses knowledge. It is a kind of cultivated gentleness. It is foreign to harsh and boisterous frontiers and comes after many of the wild creatures to which it is directed have been destroyed.
—*The Voice of the Coyote*

Sympathy for Wild Animals

Brotherhood of the Wild

In the wilderness, one species is warned by the actions of another. The dull-eyed buffalo utilized as sentinel the nimble and sensitive antelope. The antelope doe heeded the cry of the curlew in flight near her fawn hidden in the grass; the curlew's cry might mean the approach of a coyote. The pinion jay … alerts the buck against stalkers with guns. The wild turkey takes note of every squirrel bark, every rustle of leaves by the armadillo, every caw of the crow.

—*The Voice of the Coyote*

DODSLEY, ROBERT (1703–1764)
English poet, playwright and one of the most important publishers and booksellers of the eighteenth century.

Trees in Season

… the tree which appears too forward to exult in the first favorable glance of spring, will ever be the readiest to droop beneath the frowns of winter.

—*"The Oak and the Sycamore"*
from The Great Fables

DONNE, JOHN (1571?–1631)
English poet, clergymen and dean of St. Paul's Cathedral

To Reach Truth

… On a huge hill,
Cragged, and steep, Truth stands, and he that will
Reach her, about must go, and about must go;

—*Satyre III*

Love built on beauty, soon as beauty, dies,
> —*Elegies, No. 2, The Anagram*

Love's Demise

EDMAN, IRWIN (1896–1954)
Philosopher, poet and professor of philosophy,
Columbia University

We are deluged with facts, but it is principles people are looking for ... it is ideas, even ideals, that are sought. And what is required is the note of conviction and contagion of counsel that will turn anarchy into meaning, into order.
> —*Under Whatever Sky*

*What People
Are Looking For*

It may be said ... that the essence of being adult rather than childish is to cease to be sulky and irritable at finding life and existence to be what they are. It means among other things to be able to face life steadily and without illusion—but also without disillusion. ...
> —*Adams: The Baby and the Man from Mars*

*The Essence
of Being Adult*

EDWARDS, JONATHAN (1703–1758)
New England clergyman, philosopher, preacher
and revivalist in Colonial America

Surely there is something in the unruffled calm of nature that overawes our little anxieties and doubts: the sight of the deep-blue sky, and the clustering stars above, seem to impart a quiet to the mind.
> —*The New Dictionary of Thoughts*

Nature's Calming Effect

EISELEY, LOREN (1907–1977)

American author, poet, anthropologist and teacher; winner of the John Burroughs Medal for *The Firmament of Time* (1961)

"Fragmenting" Man

January 28, 1956

Man is always marveling at what he has blown apart, never at what the universe has put together, and this is his limitation. He still has something of the destructive primate mind within him. He is at heart a "fragmenting" creature. He resents even Bergson's indeterminism and would see evolution as the response of the dead to the dead—not indeterminate at all. Man, the creation of the universe, after all created the bomb.

—*The Lost Notebooks of Loren Eiseley*

A Reverence for Life

No, it is not because I am filled with obscure guilt that I step gently over, and not upon, an autumn cricket. It is not because of guilt that I refuse to shoot the last osprey from her nest in the tide marsh. I possess empathy; I have grown with man in his mind's growing. I share that sympathy and compassion which extends beyond the barriers of class and race and form until it partakes of the universal whole. I am not ashamed to profess this emotion, nor will I call it a pathology. Only through this experience many times repeated and enhanced does man become truly human. Only then will his gun arm be forever lowered. I pray that it may sometime be so.

—*The Lost Notebooks of Loren Eiseley*

ELLWANGER, GEORGE H. (dates unknown)
Author

Books on nature ... are no exception in their lasting qualities to those on numerous other subjects; their permanence depends upon the man rather than upon the topic.
—*"Critical and Biographical Introduction" to the Natural History of Selborne*

What Makes a Nature Book Permanent

Analagous reasoning served White but rarely; his facts are taken at first hand, or, as he himself says, from the subject itself, and not from the writings of others. His eye was as keen as Thoreau's and Jefferies, although he lacked the vivid imaginative sense of the Walden recluse, and the intensely artistic feeling of the great essayist of the Wiltshire Downs. His modesty withal was on a par with his wonderous patience, as was equally his spirit of contentment with his lot in life.
—*"Critical and Biographical Introduction" to the Natural History of Selborne*

The Patience and Contentment of Gilbert White

EMERSON, RALPH WALDO (1803–1882)
American essayist, poet, philosopher and lecturer

I find nothing in fables more astonishing than my experience in every hour. One moment of a man's life is a fact so stupendous as to take the lustre out of all fiction.
—*Demonology, Lectures and Biographical Sketches*

Human Life— The Greatest Fable

The Art of Quotation

... people quote so differently: one finding only what is gaudy and popular; another, the heart of the author, the report of his select and happiest hour. ... We are as much informed of a writer's genius by what he selects as by what he originates. We read the quotation with his eyes and find a new and fervent sense; as a passage from one of the poets, well recited, borrows new interest from the rendering. ... The profoundest thought or passion sleeps as in a mine until an equal mind and heart finds and publishes it.

—*"Quotation and Originality"*

Man and Dog

You may catch the glance of a dog sometimes which seems to lay a kind of claim to sympathy and brotherhood. What! somewhat of me down there? Does the dog know it? Can he, too, as I, go out of himself, see himself, perceive relations? We fear lest they should catch a glimpse of his condition, should learn in some moment the tough limitations of this fettering organization. It was in this glance that Ovid got the hint of his metamorphoses; Calidrea of his transmigration of souls.

—*Lectures and Biographical Sketches*

The Power of Enthusiasm

Every great and commanding moment in the annals of the world is the triumph of some enthusiasm.

—*Nature Addresses and Lectures*

Why We Love Nature

... Nature is loved by what is best in us. It is loved as the city of God, ... rather because there is no citizen.

—*Nature*

A beautiful soul dwells always in a beautiful world.

—*Society and Solitude*

Beauty Sees Beauty

If my garden had only made me acquainted with the muck-worm, the bugs, the grasses, and the swamp of plenty in August, I should willingly pay a free tuition. But every process is lucrative to me far beyond its economy.

—*Society and Solitude*

The Harvest of Emerson's Garden

The inhabitants of cities suppose that the country landscape is pleasant only half the year. I please myself with observing the graces of the winter scenery, and believe that we are as much touched by it as by the genial influences of summer. To the attentive eye, each moment of the year has its own beauty, and in the same field, it beholds, every hour, a picture which was never seen before, and which shall never be seen again. ...

—*"Beauty"*
Nature Addresses and Lectures

Beauty in All Hours

Every man takes care that his neighbor shall not cheat him. But a day comes when he begins to care that he does not cheat his neighbor. Then all goes well. He has changed his market-cart into a chariot of the sun.

—*From an Essay,*
Worship, Conduct of Life

The Day of Faith

I am content and occupied with such miracles as I know, such as my eyes and ears daily show me. ...

—*Demonology, Lectures and Biographical Sketches*

The Daily Miracles

How to Enjoy
the Country

... The first care of a man settling in the country should be to open the face of the earth to himself by a little knowledge of Nature, or a great deal, if he can; of birds, plants, rocks, astronomy; in short, the art of taking a walk. This will draw the sting out of frost, dreariness out of November and March, and the drowsiness out of August.

—*Resources*

Experience and
Instinctive Knowledge

... what one man is said to learn by experience, a man of extraordinary sagacity is said, without experience, to divine. The Arabians say that Abul Khan, the mystic, and Abu Ali Seena, the philosopher, conferred together; and, on parting, the philosopher said, "All that he sees, I know," and the mystic said, "All that he knows, I see."

—*Swedenborg, or, The Mystic*

Wonders in
Common Things

The invariable mark of wisdom is to see the miraculous in the common. ... To the wise, therefore, a fact is true poetry, and the most beautiful of fables. ...

—*From an Essay, "Prospects,"
Nature Addresses and Lectures*

Seeing Beauty in
All Wild Things

A squirrel leaping from bough to bough and making the wood but one wide tree for his pleasure, fills the eye not less than a lion, is beautiful, self-sufficing, and stands then and there for nature.

—*From an essay, "Art in Essays,"
First Series*

... To the body and mind which have been cramped by noxious work or company, nature is medicinal and restores their tone. The tradesman, the attorney comes out of the din and craft of the street and sees the sky and the woods, and is a man again. In their eternal calm, he finds himself. ...

—From an essay, "Beauty"
Nature Addresses and Lectures

Our Need for Sky and Woods

Not he is great who can alter matter, but he who can alter my state of mind. They are the kings of the world who give the color of their present thought to all nature and all art, and persuade men by the cheerful serenity of their carrying the matter, that this thing which they do is the apple which the ages have desired to pluck, now at last ripe, and inviting nations to the harvest.

—The American Scholar

The Kings of the World

Be content with a little light,
So be it your own.
Explore, and explore

—Literary Ethics

A Little Light

EURIPIDES (480–405 B.C.)
Greek tragic playwright

Happy the man whose lot it is to know
The secrets of the earth. He hastens not
To work his fellows hurt by unjust deeds,
But with rapt admiration contemplates
Immortal Nature's ageless harmony,
And how and when her order came to be.

The Happy Naturalist

EVANS, HOWARD SIGNAL (1919–)
American entomologist, author,
educator and professor of entomology

*Our Little-Studied
Insects*

    The greatest of all sources of pleasure is
discovery. Given a plot of earth, whether in a
suburban garden, a prairie, or a rain forest, it
will be ... crowded with insects. There are ...
many levels of discovery. The first seasonal
report: the first swallowtail of spring, crossing
the backyard. The first personal discovery:
perhaps a two-spotted ladybeetle devouring rose
aphids. The first regional record: perhaps a
Carolina mantid in Montana. Or, of course,
something wholly new to science: a new host
relationship, new insights on behavior, fresh
knowledge on details of life histories. Most
estimates have it that only about half the
existing species of insects have yet been named
and described: most of these are in the tropics,
but not all ... there are currently intensive
research programs on such commonplace insects
as hornworms, blister beetles, and honey bees.
The air and the bushes are full of wholly
unstudied insect species. There seems no end of
what may still be learned, and all of what we
learn will have a bearing on our ultimate success
in coexisting with insects.

                —*The Pleasures of Entomology*

FABRE, JEAN HENRI (1823–1915)
French entomologist and author

When we lack the society of our fellowmen, we take refuge in that of animals, without always losing by the change.
—*The Wonders of Instinct*

The Friendship of Animals

A day will come ... when, after making progress upon progress, man will succumb, destroyed by the excess of what he calls civilization. Too eager to play the god, he cannot hope for the animal's placid longevity; he will have disappeared when the little Toad is still saying his litany, in company with the Grasshopper, the Scops-owl and the others. They were singing on this planet before us; they will sing after us, celebrating what can never change, the fiery glory of the sun.
—*The Wonders of Instinct*

Civilization— The Destroyer

We have all of us, men and animals, some special gift. One child takes to music, another is always modeling things in clay; another is quick at figures. It is the same way with insects. One kind of Bee can cut leaves; another builds clay houses, Spiders know how to make webs. These gifts exist because they exist, and that is all any one can say. In human beings we call the special gift genius. In an insect we call it instinct. Instinct is the animal's genius.
—*Insect Adventures*

The "Gifts" of Men and Animals

Animals—The Consolation of Old Age

We never know what will happen to us. Mathematics on which I spent so much time in my youth, has been of hardly any good to me; and animals, which I avoided as much as ever I could, are the consolation of my old age.

—*Insect Adventures*

The Lantern-bearer

Few insects ... vie in popular fame with the Glow-worm, that curious little animal which, to celebrate the little joys of life, kindles a beacon at its tail-end. Who does not know it, at least by name? Who has not seen it roam amid the grass, like a spark fallen from the moon at full? The Greeks of old called it ... the bright-tailed. Science ... calls it the lantern-bearer. ...

—*The Wonders of Instinct*

Gross Feeding Brutalizes

Frugality ... softens character, in animals as in men; gross feeding brutalizes it. The gormandizer gorged with meat and strong drink, a fruitful source of savage outbursts, could not possess the gentleness of the ascetic who dips his bread into a cup of milk.

—*The Wonders of Instinct*

The Beauty of Truth

Even when poorly clad, truth is still beautiful.

—*The Wonders of Instinct*

What History Does Not Tell Us

History ... celebrates the battle-fields whereon we meet our death, but scorns to speak of the plowed fields whereby we thrive; it knows the names of the king's bastards but cannot tell us the origin of wheat.

—*The Wonders of Instinct*

Animals are a little like ourselves: they excel in an art only on condition of specializing in it.

—*The Wonders of Instinct*

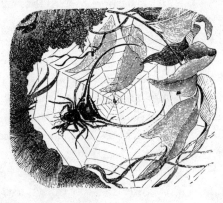

FADIMAN, CLIFTON (1904–   )
Writer, editor, TV entertainer and master of ceremonies on "Information Please" radio show (1938–1948)

The lackluster face of the subway rider reading his newspaper, the vacant look of the moviegoer emerging from his dark cave, the unexpectant countenances of the citizens swarming along Broadway: these are all pictures of a special boredom. Not unhappiness, not fatigue, and certainly not aristocratic ennui; but that old modern *stunned* look that comes of a surfeit of toys and a deficiency of thoughts.

—*Boredom, Brainstorms and Bombs*

Signs of Our Special Boredom

We delude ourselves into thinking that because we know a thing we think we have done something about it: our equivalent of the primitive's belief that to name is to control.

—*Boredom, Brainstorms and Bombs*

Our Modern Delusion

Birds—Our
Musical Poets

FISHER, JAMES (1912–   )
English ornithologist, conservationist, author and educator

... Charles Hartshorne seems the first to have had the courage to suggest in a scientific journal that birds are proprietors of a primitive form of music. ... That no serious mainstream scientist and behavior student would really admit, indeed positively demonstrate, that bird song could be a form of art until 1958, proves the point that poets' intuition may sometimes reach the truth sooner than the searching of scientists.

For years the bird-song analysts had been overwhelmed (and correctly—first things first) with the detection and diagnosis of the biological function of song. ... Now the musical, artistic superstructure is also conceded. Birds are, or some may be, musical poets, as the bird lovers from Aristotle ... to Keats and Clare have been trying to tell us. It is probably that birds have been musicians for about a third of the geological life of their Class. ...
—*The Shell Bird Book*

The "Useless" Things
in Nature

After years of preaching by Audubonites and their equivalent in other lands, the cult of the useless is coming to power—useless flowers, useless butterflies, useless warblers and singing birds, useless hawks, useless forests, useless wilderness: all the useless things that by their very uselessness are useful ... redeeming and refreshing and needful to the human spirit. In the forefront stride the ornithologists, acolytes of gloriously useless animals whose going would leave the world a colorless and silent place.
—*The World of Birds*

FLAGLER, HENRY MORRISON (1830–1913)
Builder of Florida railroad and resort hotels

There has never been anything worth
obtaining without grief, or suffering, and disap-
pointment.

> —*Quoted in*
> *The World of The Great White Heron*
> *by Marjory Bartlett Sanger*

The Price We Pay

GARY, ROMAIN (1914–1980)
Russian-born French novelist and diplomat

... If the world can no longer afford the
luxury of natural beauty, then it will soon be
overcome and destroyed by its own ugliness. I
myself feel deeply that the fate of Man, and his
dignity, are at stake whenever the earth's
natural splendors are threatened with extinc-
tion. ... We are forever condemned to be part of
a mystery that neither logic nor imagination can
fathom, and your presence among us carries a
resonance that cannot be accounted for in terms
of science or reason, but only in terms of awe,
wonder, and reverence. You are our last innocence.

> —"*A Love Letter to an Old Companion*"

To the Wild Elephant—
Our Last Innocence

GAY, JOHN (1685–1732)
English poet, playwright and satirist

And, what's a butterfly? At best,
He's but a caterpillar drest;
> —*The Butterfly and the Snail*

The Naked Butterfly

89

**The Shepherd's Dog
and the Wolf**

"Friend," says the wolf, "the matter weigh;
Nature design'd us beasts of prey;
As such, when hunger finds a treat,
'Tis necessary Wolves should eat.

A Wolf eats Sheep but now and then,
Ten thousands are devour'd by men.
An open foe may prove a curse
But a pretended friend is worse."
—*The Great Fables of All Nations*

GREY, EDWARD (1862–1933)
(VISCOUNT GREY OF FALLODON)
English diplomat, statesman, peacemaker,
author and birding enthusiast

**Country People
and Birds**

Most country people know the very common birds by name and by eye; it is remarkable that very few know them by ear.
—*The Charm of Birds*

**The Best Songsters
of Britain**

For perfection or moving quality of voice I should place the blackcap with the blackbird and the nightingale in the first class of British song-birds.
—*The Charm of Birds*

**The Song of
the Nightingale**

"Marvellous" is an epithet to be used very sparingly either of mankind or of birds; but the epithet may be conceded to the song of the nightingale.
—*The Charm of Birds*

It is song that is the most pleasing feature of bird life, but it is the last to arouse in most people any keen or intelligent attention. The reason is, no doubt, that birds offer so much that is attractive to sight, and the eye takes precedence of the ear in interesting us.

—*The Charm of Birds*

Our Neglect of Bird Song

HAGEN, WALTER (1892–1969)
American golfing champion

You're only here for a short visit,
Don't hurry, don't worry,
And stop to smell the flowers
Along the way.

—*Quoted in TV Play*

Stop to Smell the Flowers

91

The Security of
the Universe

HALLE JR., LOUIS J. (1910–   )
Author and educator; winner of the John
Burroughs Medal for *Birds Against Man* (1941)

The migratory passage of birds, like the
movements of the stars, can be a great consolation to men whose minds continually search for
an established order and progression in the
universe. The knowledge that, whatever we may
make of ourselves in the moment of our existence, the stars will continue in their appointed
courses, the seasons will move in their con-
firmed order, the birds will pursue their destined
biannual migrations, carries with it a sense of
ultimate security which the works of man alone
fail to convey. It seems to give us the intimation
of a will that directs us, it belies our orphaned
estate in the universe. Order, harmony, regular-
ity, those elements implicit in the recurrent
flight of birds, are beyond the touch of the good
and evil that men do in the numbered hours of
their survival. Knowledge of the integrated
pattern of the universe in which the birds share,
of the final cosmic autocracy whose imposed
limits no organism may transcend, secures us
from the nightmare of anarchy.

—*Birds Against Men*

HARRIS, SYDNEY J. (1917–1986)
Newspaper columnist

What Sentimentality Is

"Sentimentality" is the name we give to any
sentiment we are incapable of feeling.

—*Quoted in Look Magazine*

HEINRICH, BERND (1940–   )

American biologist, writer, assistant professor at the University of California (1971–78); professor of entomology (1978–80); professor of zoology at the University of Vermont (1980–   ); a recipient of the National Science Foundation Grant (1971) and the American Book Award Nomination for *Bumblebee Economics*

The Commitment

Taking an animal from the wild is something one does not do casually. It requires much time and commitment to live with another creature, and one must be prepared to provide not only for its physical needs but also for its psychological requirements. With a fellow human, we can take intelligence and understanding for granted; we can verbalize our feelings or make symbolic gestures to define our relationships. With animals, however, we can never assume that they have the sense or ability to tell us what they need or want. We must study them closely for signs of their needs, and then we must make ourselves available to minister to those needs. The animal lives one day at a time and depends on its human "master," and so to have one is a constant commitment.

—*One Man's Owl*

Difficulty in Writing About Wilderness

HOAGLAND, EDWARD (1932–   )
American author

The trouble with writing about the wilderness is that there is almost none of it left, and so, although more and more writers are born, grow up and appear in print, fewer and fewer can possibly have had even an approximate acquaintance with the wild destroyed world on whose splinters we stand on.

—*Review of Black Sun*, New York Times
Sunday Book Review, *June 13, 1971*

HUBBARD, HARLAN (dates unknown)
Painter, musician, writer, shantyboater on the Ohio River for more than twenty years and author of *Payne Hollow: Life on the Fringe of Society.*

Birds' Songs at Dusk

Now I look down over the garden, past the gangling locust trees, past the leafy borders of the river and over the calm water to the shore and hills beyond, already facing into the cool gray of evening. … The sky still glows with warm light, its colors and formless clouds dimmed by the thick air of stormy June. … The evening chorus of birds has diminished, but the wood thrush's full song drifts down the hollow, as if from a celestial region far above. It ceases as the light fades and only the peewee carries on in the silence, his timid whistle expanding and rising into ecstasy, a burst of joy in the face of approaching darkness. The quiet becomes more intense. Crickets chirp faintly, then a frog down in the creek strums tentative chords and day passes into night.

—*Payne Hollow*

HUDSON, WILLIAM HENRY (1841–1922)
English naturalist, nature writer and novelist

The villager, as a rule, is not a good observer, which is not strange, since no person is,
or ever can be, a good observer of the things in
which he is not specially interested: conse-
quently the countryman only knows the most
common and the most conspicuous species. He
plods through life with downcast eyes and a
vision somewhat dimmed by indifference;
forgetting as he progresses, the small scrap of
knowledge he acquired by looking sharply
during the period of boyhood, when every living
creature excited his attention.
—*Birds in Town and Village*

*The English Villagers
Indifference to Nature*

I should say, from my own observation, that
all songsters are interested in the singing of
other species, ... in certain notes, especially the
most striking in power, beauty, and strangeness.
Thus, when the cuckoo starts calling, you will
see other small birds fly straight to the tree and
perch near him, apparently to listen. ... And
among the listeners you will find the sparrow
and tits of various species which are never
victimized by the cuckoo. ... Again, it is my
experience that, when a nightingale starts
singing, the small birds near immediately
become attentive, often suspending their own
songs. And some flying to perch near him, and
listen, just as they listen to the cuckoo.
—*Birds in Town and Village*

The Bird Listeners

The Green Mistress

For my mistress is more to me than any Cynthia to any poet; she is immortal and has green hair and green eyes, and her body and soul are green, and to those who live with and love her she gives a green soul as a special favour.

—*Adventures Among Birds*

One Flower Among Thousands

On looking on a meadow, yellow with buttercups I have seen one flower, or a single petal, far out, perhaps, in the middle of the fields, which instantly caught and kept my sight—one flower amongst a thousand thousand flowers, all alike. It was because it had caught and reflected the light at such an angle that its yellow enamelled surface shone and sparkled like a piece of burnished gold.

—*Adventures Among Birds*

A Glorified Song of a Whinchat

... I was walking across a furze-grown common after dark on a very cold windy evening in early April when ... a whinchat warbled the fullest, sweetest song I ever listened to from that bird. After a brief interval the song was repeated, then once again. Whether it was the exceeding purity of the sound, so clear, so wondrously sweet, so unexpected at that hour, or the darkness and silence of that solitary place which gave it an almost preternatural beauty I cannot say, but the effect on me was so great that I have never walked by night in spring in any furzy place without pausing ... with the pleased expectation of hearing it again.

—*Adventures Among Birds*

... a little bird when moulting concealed in a thick shrubbery, has no heart to sing: ...
—*Adventures Among Birds*

A Bird Molting

Goats exhibit more character than sheep, probably because we do not compel them to live in a crowd.
—*The Book of a Naturalist*

The Character of Goats

And the chinchilla, white and pale gray, with round leaflike ears, and soft dove's eyes—a rare and delicate creature. There is in this small mountain troglodyte something poetic, tender, flower–like—a mammalian *edelweiss*.
—*The Book of a Naturalist*

The Chinchilla

The gardener, like the gamekeeper, is never a person who will allow you to teach him anything, ...
—*The Book of a Naturalist*

Gardeners and Gamekeepers

... unless the soul goes out to meet what we see we do not see it; nothing do we see, not a beetle, not a blade of grass.
—*The Book of a Naturalist*

Seeing Nature with the Soul

Death by accident is common enough in wild life, and a good proportion of such deaths are due to an error of judgment, often so slight as not to seem an error at all.
—*The Book of a Naturalist*

Death in the Wild

What one reads does not inform the mind much unless one observes and thinks for oneself at the same time.
—*The Book of a Naturalist*

The Value of Reading

Weed-killers

... weed-killers are even more potent than I had thought them. As a bird-lover I had always hated them on account of their destructiveness to the small birds of the homestead, the blackbird and song thrush. ...

—*The Book of a Naturalist*

Killing the Creatures We Love

I know good naturalists who have come to hate the very sight of a gun, simply, because that useful instrument has become associated in their case with the thought and memory ... of killing the creatures we love, whose secrets we wish to find out.

—*The Book of a Naturalist*

A Rule of Wildlife

It is a rule in wild life that nothing is attempted which is not perfectly safe, though to us the action may appear dangerous ... or even impossible.

—*The Book of a Naturalist*

The Charm of Discovery

Never a season passes, never a month nor a week, nor even a day, when I am wandering in quest of the sights and sounds that draw the field naturalist, but I stumble on something notable never previously seen, or never seen in the same charming aspect. And the fact that it is stumbled on when not looked for, that it comes as a complete surprise, greatly enhances the charm. It may be a bird or mammal, or some rare or lustrous insect, but it is in plant life where the happy discoveries are most frequent, even to one who ... knows little of their science. ...

—*The Book of a Naturalist*

When it is spring I walk in sheltered places, by wood and hedgeside, to look for and welcome the first comers. Oh those first flowers so glad to be alive and out in the sun and wind once more—their first early ineffable spring freshness, remembrancers of our lost childhood, dead and lost these many dim and sorrowful years, now recovered with the flowers, and immortal once more with spring's immortality!

The First Flowers of Spring

—*The Book of a Naturalist*

The bird-watcher's life is an endless succession of surprises. Almost every day he appears fated to witness some habit, some action, which he had never seen or heard of before and will perhaps never see again. ...

The Bird-watcher's Surprises

—*The Book of a Naturalist*

One of the most delightful, the most exhilarating spectacles of wild bird life is that of the soaring heron. The great blue bird, with great round wings so measured in their beats, yet so buoyant in the vast void air! It is indeed a sight which moves all men to admiration in all countries which the great bird inhabits; ...

The Flight of the Heron

—*The Book of a Naturalist*

HULL, CORDELL (1871–1955)
American statesman, winner of the Nobel Prize for peace (1945) and secretary of state (1933–1944)

A lie will gallop half-way around the world
While Truth is pulling its breeches on.

Slow Truths

HUXLEY, JULIAN (1887–1975)
English biologist, writer, lecturer, evolutionist and scholar

Improvement Through Evolution

Living substance demonstrates its improvement during evolution by doing old things in new and better ways, by acquiring new properties, by organizing itself in new forms, by increasing its efficiency and enlarging its variety.
—*Evolution in Action*

The Miracle of Mind

The miracle of mind is that it can transmute quantity into quality. This property of mind is something given: it just is so. It cannot be explained: it can only be accepted.
—*Evolution in Action*

HUXLEY, THOMAS (1825–1895)
English biologist, teacher, lecturer and popularizer of science known for his defense of the theory of evolution held by Darwin

The Nature of a Man

Men, my dear, are very queer animals, a mixture of horse-nervousness, ass-stubbornness and camel-malice—with an angel bobbing about unexpectedly ... and when they can do exactly as they please, they are very hard to drive.
—*Life and Letters of Thomas H. Huxley*

JACKSON, HOLBROOK (1874–1948)
English literary scholar and editor

Emerson corrected what he saw by what he thought, as Thoreau corrected what he thought by what he saw, and it is probable that he realised more exactly than Emerson the difference between perception and observation. Observation for Thoreau is seeing without compromise ... "How to observe is how to behave. We are as much as we see." And his whole attitude towards life emphasizes the importance of first-sight or freshness of vision. "The most poetic and truest account of objects is generally given those who first observe them, or the discoverers of them."

Thoreau's Freshness of Vision

—*The Reading of Books*

The artist is like a child in so far as he sees things for the first time. But no child remains for long in a state of wonder. Children are realists, not artists, and soon weary of the latest wonderment. To carry on the feelings of childhood into the powers of manhood: to combine the child's sense of wonder and novelty with the appearances, which every day for perhaps forty years had rendered familiar ... this is the character of genius.

The Character of Genius

—*The Reading of Books*

JEFFERIES, RICHARD (1848–1887)
English naturalist and novelist

Hours of Beauty

The hours when the mind is absorbed by beauty are the only hours when we really live, ...
—*The Life of the Fields*

Where Thought Dwells

Thought dwells by the stream and sea, by the hill and in the woodland, in the sunlight and free wind, where the wild dove haunts.
—*The Life of the Fields*

Seeing the Things Around Us

Open your eyes and see those things which are around us at this hour.
—*The Life of the Fields*

The Wild Bumblebee
(*"humble-bee" in England*)

... No one cares for the humble-bee. But down to the flowering nettle in the mossy-sided ditch, up into the tall elm, winding in and out and round the branched buttercups, along the banks of the brook, far inside the deepest wood, away he wanders and despises nothing. ... Humble he is, but wild; always in the field, the wood, always by the banks and thickets: always wild and humming to his flowers. ...
—*The Life of the Fields*

Living in Remoteness

Those who have lived all their lives in remote places do not feel the remoteness.
—*The Life of the Fields*

The Winds of the Hills

Those who desire air and quick recovery should go to the hills, where the wind has a scent of the sunbeams.
—*The Life of the Fields*

It is the peculiarity of knowledge that those who really thirst for it always get it.
> —*The Life of the Fields*

Those Who Thirst for Knowledge

The sunlight and the winds enter London, and the life of the fields is there too, if you will but see it.
> —*The Life of the Fields*

Sunlight in London

An endless succession of labour ... it is a sadness ... this ceaseless labour, repeating the furrow, reiterating the blow, the same furrow, the same stroke. ... shall we never know how to lighten it, how to live with the flowers, the swallows, the sweet delicious shade, and the murmur of the stream?
> —*The Life of the Fields*

The Sadness of Farm Labor

Till it has been painted and sung by poet, and described by writers, nothing is human.
> —*The Life of the Fields*

To Make Something Human

... Consider the grasses and the oaks, the swallows, the sweet blue butterfly—they are one and all a sign and token showing before our eyes earth made into life. ... There is so much for us yet to come, so much to be gathered, and enjoyed. Not for you or me, now, but for our race, who will ultimately use this magical secret for their happiness. ...
> —*The Life of the Fields*

A Secret for Happiness

Why Country People Walk Slowly

... you cannot walk fast very long in a footpath; no matter how rapidly at first, you soon lessen your pace, and so country people always walk slowly.

—*The Life of the Fields*

Birds and Fly-Fishing

It is the birds and other creatures peculiar to the water that render fly-fishing so pleasant; were they all destroyed, and nothing left but the mere fish, one might as well stand and fish in a stone cattle-trough.

—*The Life of the Fields*

Lost Leaves

The lost leaves measure our years; they are gone as the days are gone, and the bare branches silently speak of a new year, ...

—*The Life of the Fields*

The Ideal of Nature

To be beautiful and to be calm, without mental fear, is the ideal of nature.

—*The Life of the Fields*

Life Lengthens in Summer

Not only the days, but life itself lengthens in summer. I would spread abroad my arms and gather more of it to me, could I do so.

—*The Life of the Fields*

The Cleverness of Fish

I deny altogether that the cold-blooded fish ... is stupid, or slow to learn. On the contrary, fish are remarkably quick, not only under natural conditions, but quick at accommodating themselves to altered circumstances which they could not foresee, ...

—*The Life of the Fields*

I never see roads, or horses, men or anything when I get beside a brook.

—*The Life of the Fields*

The Spell of a Brook

There seems always a depth, somewhere, unexplored, a thicket that has not been seen through, a corner full of ferns, a quaint old hollow tree, which may give us something.

—*The Life of the Fields*

Nature's Perennial Lure

… Without hedges England would not be England. Hedges, thick and high, and full of flowers, birds and living creatures, of shade and flecks of sunshine dancing up and down. … You do not know how much there is in hedges.

—*The Life of the Fields*

The Beauty of Hedges

If but by reason and will I could reach the godlike calm and courage of what we so thoughtlessly call the timid turtle-dove, I should lead a nearly perfect life.

—*The Life of the Fields*

The Calm and Courage of the Turtle-Dove

Without the blackbird, in whose throat the sweetness of the green fields dwells, the days would be only partly summer.

—*The Life of the Fields*

Without the Blackbird

… So concentrated on their little work in the sunshine, so intent on the tiny egg, on the insect captured on the grass–tip to be carried to the eager fledglings, so joyful in listening to the song poured out for them or in pouring it forth. … If they could only live longer! …

—*The Life of the Fields*

The Shortness of Birds' Lives

JOHNSON, SAMUEL (1709–1784)
English lexicographer, essayist, poet and moralist

A Time to Write

A man may write at anytime if he will set himself doggedly to it.
—*The Penny Classics*

Curiosity—
A Sign of Intellect

Curiosity is one of the permanent and certain characteristics of a vigorous intellect. Every advance into knowledge opens new prospects and produces new incitements to further progress.
—*The Penny Classics*

KEATS, JOHN (1795–1821)
English poet

To Become a
Part of Nature

The setting sun will always set me aright …
… if a sparrow come before my window, I take part in his existence and pick about in the gravel …
—*Letters of John Keats to His Family and Friends*

KEMPIS, THOMAS À. (C. 1380–1471)
(THOMAS HAMERKEN VON KEMPEN)
German monk and writer, author of *The Imitation of Christ*

Every Creature a
Mirror of Life

If indeed thy heart were right, then would every creature be to thee a mirror of life, and a book of holy doctrine.
—*Adaptive Coloration of Animals*

KIERAN, JOHN (1892–1981)

Writer, columnist, ornithologist, scholar and member of panel of TV's "Information Please"; winner of the John Burroughs Medal for *Natural History of New York City* (1960)

As we sat there on long summer evenings with twilight slowly deepening into dusk, a Whip-poor-will came regularly to sit on a smooth stone quite close to us and bob its head as it uttered its vibrant call: "Whip-poor-WILL! Whip-poor-WILL! Whip-poor-WILL." There was a wild, forlorn, plaintive touch to it that made such a lasting impression on me that if I hear the bird now in the dusk, I am a boy again sitting in a meadow at twilight with my farmer friend, the filly grazing nearby, and the Whip-poor-will is calling to me out of the mist of vanished years.

The Cry of the Whip-poor-will

—*Footnotes on Nature*

Pasture land makes easy walking. The cows and horses pave the way. ... They keep the grass cropped short and they make paths through the gullies and along the steep hillsides.

Walking in Pasture Land

—*Footnotes on Nature*

It probably is true that a man sees more things and makes more searching observations in the field when he is alone, but there is a virtue in companionship that makes up for any decrease in the supply of clinical notes. A pleasure shared is a pleasure doubled. I always like to have companions on my tramps through the woods, my walks through the fields or my trips to the seashore.

The Virtue of Companionship in the Field

—*Footnotes on Nature*

Packing Apples

What finer occupation is there in the wide world than that of packing apples of a bright Autumn day with a light west wind blowing and scattered white clouds floating fleecily across the deep blue sky?

—*Footnotes on Nature*

KILHAM, LAWRENCE (1910–)
Graduate of Harvard Medical School and writer-naturalist internationally known for his studies of behavior of birds and other animals; winner of the John Burroughs Medal for *On Watching Birds* (1989)

A Way to Keep Alive

One of the saddest things in science is to see scientists who have run out of things to do. The way to keep alive, whether as a scientist or an amatuer, is to maintain interests in many things.

—*On Watching Birds*

The Substance in Some Older Authors

It sometimes surprises me to hear young professional or other ornithologists speak with scorn of any reference that is at all old. I myself tend toward the reverse assumption, finding at times more substance, individuality, and inventiveness in older authors than in modern ones. ...

—*On Watching Birds*

How the Watcher Grows

Behavior watching is cumulative, and when one gets the knack of it, the more one sees and reflects, the more one is apt to observe. And reading, creative reading of the kind that generates ideas and sparks enthusiasm, can be a great asset if you want to keep right on through old age.

—*On Watching Birds*

KIPLING, RUDYARD (1865–1936)
English novelist, poet and short-story writer

I keep six honest serving men,	*Six Serving Men*
They taught me all I know	
Their names are What and Why and When	
And Where and Who and How.	

       —*Just So Stories*

There was never a King like Solomon	*Solomon's Secret*
Not since the world began,	
Yet Solomon talked to a butterfly	
As a man would talk to a man.	

     —*The Man Who Talked to Animals*

KRUTCH, JOSEPH WOOD (1893–1970)
American critic, naturalist, essayist, teacher and
nature writer; winner of the John Burroughs
Medal for *The Desert Year* (1954)

Joy in Bird Song

  The ornithologist who has convinced
himself that bird song "has nothing to do" with
joy has not taken anything away from the robin.
Ornithology notwithstanding, the robin continues to pour forth his heart in profuse strains of
unpremeditated art. But such an ornithologist
has taken a good deal away from himself and
from those who feel constrained to believe him.
They have forced themselves to live in a world
that has come to seem, not joyful, but joyless.
Robins and cardinals know better.

       —*The Great Chain of Life*

Ants—Before Man

If, as the anthropologists believe, man has been a social animal for not more than a million years then certain insects discovered the advantages of a cooperating group something like thirty million years before he did and our progenitors might profitably have heeded an injunction "go to the ant," not so much to learn industry as to learn the agriculture and the animal husbandry man had not yet dreamed of.
—*The Great Chain of Life*

Animals' Awareness and Emotions

Somehow or other awareness means not only intellectual grasp but also emotional involvement. Both either first came into being or at least first became a conspicuous part of a living creature's existence a very long time ago, though not when life itself began. And from the human standpoint emotional involvement is quite as important as intellectual grasp. Even the animals with which we live most intimately, the dog and the cat, bewilder us when we try to understand their minds. They seem sometimes so intelligent, so understanding; at other times so incapable of grasping a situation that seems to us so overwhelmingly obvious. We never quite know what to make of them when we consider them as intellectually our kin. Often we wonder whether in our sense they can think at all, and a great gulf opens between us. But it is clear enough that they share our emotions even though they cannot share our thoughts. And it is not merely that they are glad or sad. We see them also jealous, hurt, sometimes ashamed. And here again the touch of nature which makes us kin is not intellectual but emotional.
—*The Great Chain of Life*

Both Wordsworth and Thoreau knew that when the light of common day seemed no more than common it was because of something lacking in them, not because of something lacking in it, and what they asked for was eyes to see a universe they knew was worth seeing. For that reason theirs are the best of all attempts to describe what real awareness consists of … that the rare moment is not the moment when there is something worth looking at but the moment when we are capable of seeing it.

—*The Desert Year*

What Real Awareness Is

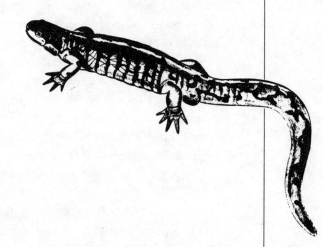

Personally, I feel both happier and more secure when I am reminded that I have the backing of something older and perhaps more permanent than I am—the something, I mean, which taught the flower to count five and the beetle to know that spots are more pleasing if arranged in a definite order. Some of the most important secrets are, they assure me, known to others than myself.

—*The Best of Two Worlds*

One Naturalist's Security

Nature and the Farmer

Country schools now give courses in "nature study" to the farmers' children, and they often need them almost as much as those bred in cities. Your farmer frequently grows up in an ignorance (the maintenance of which it seems difficult to understand) of everything in nature not immediately relevant to his profession. More than once—and plainly rather out of politeness to me than because of any genuine curiosity—I have been summoned to wonder at some creature described as strange, horrendous, and undoubtedly extremely rare, only to have it turn out a prevalent insect or, perhaps, one of the commonest of the salamanders. And how sinister everything not a regular part of his daily life seems to be! Every milksnake is a copperhead, every spider is deadly, nearly every weed is poisonous. I should be willing to bet that the famous brave man who first ate an oyster came from inland and that it was not a farmer who exploded the legend of the noxious tomato.

—*The Best of Two Worlds*

Nature and the City-Dweller

Joy is the one thing of which indisputably the healthy animal, and even the healthy plant, gives us an example. And we need them to remind us that beauty and joy can come of their own accord when we let them. The geranium on the tenement window and the orchid in the florist's shop, the poodle on the leash and the goldfish in the bowl, are better than nothing. In the consciousness of the city-dweller, they ought to play a part no less essential than that of the sleek chrome chair and the Braque and Miro. For me, however, I found them not enough.

—*The Best of Two Worlds*

The animals woe—no less truly, perhaps, the animal's happiness—is unqualified by either memory or anticipation. It is a fact which fills for him the whole universe. He knows nothing of the consolation of either religion or philosophy. He cannot even say, "This also will pass." Every moment is his eternity because he cannot know that it will not last forever. If, therefore, his joy is without shadow, perhaps his being in misery is without alleviation. And that, so some might say, is what hell would be like. What other creature has ever been so miserable as an animal who has never known anything except want and abuse, and who cannot know that such a thing as kindness or even comfort exists in the universe?

—*The Best of Two Worlds*

The Animal's Eternity

LANDIS, PAUL (1901–   )
Writer

In this courageous acceptance of life as it is, the Greeks succeeded in uniting the passion for truth and the sense of wonder with a completeness to which our only modern parallel is the truly great scientific mind, which will have nothing but truth, and knows that to find truth it must accept, not judge, the facts of nature.

—*From Introduction to Four Famous Greek Plays*

To Find Truth in Nature

A Bird in the Hand

LAWRENCE, LOUISE DE KIRILINE (1894–   )
Canadian writer, ornithologist, bird-bander and
ethologist; lived with husband on Pimisi Bay, On-
tario in wilderness when writing *The Lovely and the
Wild*, the winner of the John Burroughs Medal
(1969)

To have a wild bird come to my hand of its
own free will seemed to me for a long time an
utterly remote possibility. It is different ... in
the populated areas where the animals become
conditioned to man and corrupted ... led astray
from their wild ways.

Peet was the first chickadee that introduced
itself to me. He sat on a twig and rather in fun,
expecting nothing, I offered him a sunflower
seed. To my immense surprise he alighted on my
hand, looked me in the eye, and curled his feet
around my finger. ...

I am positive that Peet was seeing this kind
of seed for the first time ... yet not only did he
recognize the seed as food, but he knew precisely
what to do with it ... opening the shell with a
series of smart taps and then with a deft twist of
the bill extracting the kernel.

Peet brought practically the whole chickadee population to my hand that first winter.

The last time Peet came to my hand he was
on his way ... to his nesting territory in the
northwest ravine.

When and how Peet died I never knew. Nor
did it matter. He disappeared, that was all.
When separation is inevitable, as it always must
be, sooner or later, this is a lovely way for a
friend to take his leave—to be there and then
just to be gone.

—The Lovely and the Wild

I know of no occupation so fulfilling as that of being a watcher. The observing self is pushed into the background. ... The present is dominated by the natural stage and all senses focused upon the amazing events that are constantly taking place.

So I sit still, absolutely still, and absorb what I can of the great play. I hear a tremendous splashing. Two deer are swimming across the bay coming this way, forging like two magnificent icebreakers through the slushy ice still floating on the surface of the partially defrosted lake. The noise they make fills the air. They land a ... hundred feet from where I am motionless. A sweet southerly breeze blows my scent the other way. Stepping daintily on cloven hoods they walk past close behind me, unperturbed, unsuspecting. The nearest one gives its head a mighty shake, an icy drop of water is catapulted unexpectedly onto my cheek. The deer climb the slope, they are in no hurry, the trees and bushes swallow them.

—*The Lovely and the Wild*

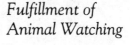

Fulfillment of Animal Watching

The Strike of the Hawk

The sound of wild alarm cries startles me. ... the warblers dash for cover ... under the thick shelter of bracken and sarsaparilla. ... The assault comes fast as lightning. The dark shadow streaks past ... I do not fully realize what is happening until I see the sharp-shinned hawk land on the rounded boulder. Under its talons a tuft of soft yellow feathers trembles in a last spasmodic shudder.

Do not disturb or distract the hawk, do not cause it to falter! What is to be done should be done fast; there is mercy in speed and surprise. For a moment the hawk remains sitting where it landed, its deep orange eyes surveying the surroundings, a proud denizen of the forest pursuing its legitimate prey. Presently the hawk lifts easily, for the tiny limp burden is light, to perform the last rite elsewhere.

—*The Lovely and the Wild*

The return of a banded bird grows more
poignant and impressive with every year that
the bird reappears, simply because it is still alive.
When the time comes, as inevitably it must, too
soon, much too soon, when I wait for it in vain,
the knowledge of the details of its life imparted
by the band that made the bearer into an
individual separated and detached from the
anonymous throng somehow mitigates the
feeling of loss. The band gave it stature and
importance as a fellow creature belonging to the
same universal cast. And in this sense the
banded bird's journey south and again north-
ward acquires a greater measure of meaning and
actuality, because the thought of this personally
known mite winging its way over such great and
hostile distances, practically alone and sometimes for the first time can now make me better
realize the immensity of this annual avian
undertaking and the proportions of its risks.

—The Lovely and the Wild

Story of the Banded Bird

LE GALLIENNE, RICHARD (1866–1947)
English poet of French descent

I meant to do my work to-day—
But a brown bird sang in the appletree,
And a butterfly flitted across the field,
And all the leaves were calling me.

And the wind went sighing over the land,
Tossing the grasses to and fro,
And a rainbow held out its shining hand—
So what could I do but laugh and go?

—The Lonely Dancer

*I Meant to Do
My Work To-day*

LEOPOLD, ALDO (1886–1948)

American author, conservationist and professor of wildlife management; winner of the John Burroughs Medal for *Sand Creek Almanac* (1977)

The Final Test of the Hunter

The common denominator of all hunters is the realization that there is always something to hunt. The world teems with creatures, processes, and events that are trying to elude you; there is always the deer, and always a swath down which he can be seen. Every ground is a hunting ground, whether it lies between you and the curbstone, or in those illimitable woods where rolls the Oregon. The final test of the hunter is whether he is keen to go hunting in a vacant lot.

—*Round River*

The Sacrifice of "Wild Things"

Like winds and sunsets, wild things were taken for granted until progress began to do away with them. Now we face the question whether a still higher "standard of living" is worth its cost in things natural, wild and free. For us of the minority, the opportunity to see geese is more important that television, and the chance to find a pasque-flower is a right as inalienable as free speech.

—*A Sand County Almanac*

Dangers in Not Owning a Farm

There are two spiritual dangers in not owning a farm. One is the danger of supposing that breakfast comes from the grocery, and the other that heat comes from the furnace.

—*A Sand County Almanac*

One swallow does not make a summer, but one skein of geese, cleaving the murk of a March thaw, is the spring.

　　　　　　—A Sand County Almanac

Wild Geese and Spring

There is a peculiar virtue in the music of elusive birds. Songsters that sing from top-most boughs are easily seen and as easily forgotten; they have the mediocrity of the obvious. What one remembers is the invisible hermit thrush pouring silver chords from impenetrable shadows; the soaring crane trumpeting from behind a cloud; the prairie chicken booming from the mists of nowhere; the quail's Ave Maria in the hush of dawn. No naturalist has even seen the choral act, for the covey is still on its invisible roost in the grass, and any attempt to approach automatically induces silence.

　　　　　　—A Sand County Almanac

The Music of Elusive Birds

Getting up too early is a vice habitual in horned owls, stars, geese and freight trains.

　　　　　　—A Sand County Almanac

Getting Up Early

I have read many definitions of what is a conservationist, and written not a few myself, but I suspect that the best one is written, not with a pen, but with an axe. It is a matter of what a man thinks about while chopping, or while deciding what to chop. A conservationist is one who is humbly aware that with each stroke he is writing his signature on the face of his land. Signatures of course differ, whether written with axe or pen, and this is as it should be.

　　　　　　—A Sand County Almanac

A Conservationist

Trees

The only conclusion I have ever reached is that I love all trees, but I am in love with pines.

—*A Sand County Almanac*

The Greatest of All Trees

To me an ancient cottonwood is the greatest of trees because in his youth he shaded the buffalo and wore a halo of pigeons, and I like a young cottonwood because he may some day become ancient. But the farmer's wife (and hence the farmer) despises all cottonwoods because in June the female tree clogs the screens with cotton. The modern dogma is comfort at any cost.

—*A Sand County Almanac*

To Plant a Pine

To plant a pine one need be neither god nor poet; one need only own a shovel.

—*A Sand County Almanac*

Quality in Nature

Our ability to perceive quality in nature begins, as in art, with the pretty. It expands through successive stages of the beautiful to values as yet uncaptured by language. ...

—*A Sand County Almanac*

The Last Crane

Someday, perhaps in the very process of our benefactions, perhaps in the fullness of geologic time, the last crane will trumpet his farewell and spiral skyward from the great marsh. High out of clouds will fall the sound of hunting horns, the baying of the phantom pack, the tinkle of little bells, and then a silence never to be broken, unless perchance in some far pasture of the Milky Way.

—*A Sand County Almanac*

Sometimes in June, when I see unearned dividends of dew hung on every lupine, I have doubts about the real poverty of the sands.
—*A Sand County Almanac*

The Poverty of Sands

... The new creek bed is ditched straight as a ruler; it has been "uncurled" by the county engineer to hurry the run-off. On the hill in the background are contoured strip-crops; they have been "curled" by the erosion engineer to retard the run-off. The water must be confused by so much advice.
—*A Sand County Almanac*

Conservation and Confusion

It must be poor life that achieves freedom from fear.
—*A Sand County Almanac*

Freedom from Fear

It is the part of wisdom never to revisit a wilderness, for the more golden the lily, the more certain that someone has gilded it. To return not only spoils a trip, but tarnishes a memory. It is only in the mind that shining adventure remains forever bright. ...
—*A Sand County Almanac*

To Tarnish a Memory

For the last word in procrastination, go travel with a river reluctant to lose his freedom in the sea.
—*A Sand County Almanac*

Procrastination

The life of every river sings its own song, but in most the song is long since marred by the discords of misuse.
—*A Sand County Almanac*

Song of the River

LONGFELLOW, HENRY WADSWORTH (1807–1882)
American poet, romancer, translator and college professor

God's Poor

The birds, God's poor who cannot wait.
—*The Sermon of St. Francis*

LONGSTRETH, T. MORRIS (1886–1975)
American author and popularizer of books about weather

Lost Wisdom

Weather was once a matter of life and death. The sailor, the hunter, and the herdsman had to read the skies aright or perish. Flood, drought, hurricane, and blizzard were not simply things that happened to somebody else's bank account. They were personal and deadly. Then came cities and steam heat ... for tens of millions the weather was something you glanced at in the papers. An urban generation lost its feeling for weather and the old racial wisdom of the wind and the rain.
—*Knowing the Weather*

The Drama of Weather

We live in a period of atmospheric turmoil. Three hundred and twenty-five volcanoes are active. The polar ice-field produce frigid and adventurous winds. The air is harried about by constantly changing pressures. The sum of these perturbations is the drama of contrasts we call weather.
—*Knowing the Weather*

There is a curiously satisfying pleasure in having an intelligent interest in the weather. There have always been those who loved it for its own sake, as born anglers love fishing regardless of the catch. These weather-lovers are part scientist, part poet. They rejoice in the forms and colors that glorify the weather. They delight in extremes. They are gratefully aware that nobody can regulate the weather, nor charge admission to it, and are happy that it is forever beyond the reach of politicians.

—*Knowing the Weather*

The Weather-Lovers

Science never wrings its hands because it has reached its last frontier. There is always some direction in which to explore.

—*Knowing the Weather*

New Frontiers

LOPEZ, BARRY (1945–   )

Writer, naturalist, wilderness traveler and contributing editor to *Harper's* and *North American Review*; winner of the John Burroughs Medal for *Of Wolves and Men* (1979), the Christopher Medal for humanitarian writing and the Pacific Northwest Book Sellers Award for excellence in nonfiction writing (1979); received an award in literature from American Academy and Institute of Arts and Letters for body of work (1986)

Our Ties to Animals

I lay there knowing something eerie ties us to the world of animals. Sometimes the animals pull you backward into it. You share hunger and fear with them like salt in the blood. Few things provoke like the presence of wild animals. They pull at us like tidal currents with questions of volition, of ethical involvement, of ancestry.

—*Arctic Dreams*

The Conversation of Death

... Wolves and prey may remain absolutely still while staring at each other. Immediately afterward, a moose may simply turn and walk away (as we saw); or the wolves may turn and run; or the wolves may charge and kill the animal in less than a minute. An intense stare is frequently used by wolves to communicate with each other, and wolves also tend to engage strangers—wolf and human—in stares. I think what transpires in those moments of staring is an exchange of information between predator and prey that either triggers a chase or defuses the hunt right there. I call this exchange the conversation of death. ...

—*Of Wolves and Men*

The wolf's howl, typically consists of a single note, rising sharply at the beginning breaking abruptly at the end. It can contain as many as twelve related harmonics. When wolves howl together they harmonize a rich, captivating sound, a seductive echo that can moan on eerily and raise the hair on your head. Wolves apparently howl to assemble the pack, especially before and after the hunt; to pass on an alarm to locate each other in a storm or in unfamiliar territory; and to communicate across great distances

What emotions prompt a howl remain unknown. ... Loneliness is the emotion most often mentioned, but group howling has a quality of celebration and camaraderie about it, what wildlife biologist Durward Allen called "the jubilation of wolves."

—*Of Wolves and Men*

Hatred and Meanness in the Human Spirit

Even today, in spite of a generally widespread sympathy for animals that have been persecuted through the ages, no more substantive reasons are needed to kill a wolf than the fact that someone feels like doing it. On a Saturday afternoon in Texas a few years ago, three men on horseback rode down a female red wolf and threw a lasso over her neck. When she gripped the rope with her teeth to keep the noose from closing, they dragged her around the prairie until they'd had broken her teeth out. Then while two of them stretched the animal between their horses with ropes, the third man beat her to death with a pair of fence pliers. The wolf was taken around to a few bars in a pickup and finally thrown in a roadside ditch.

It is relatively easy to produce reasons why such depravity exists—because people are bored, because some men feel powerless in modern society. But this incident is, in fact, a staggering act of self-indulgence. That it is condoned by silence and goes unpunished reveals a terrible meanness in the human spirit.

—*Of Wolves and Men*

Although I am familiar with wild country, I learned, I think, several remarkable things simply by walking in the woods with River and Prairie and paying attention to what they did. ... The wolves moved deftly and silently in the woods and in trying to imitate them I came to walk more quietly and to freeze at the sign of slight movement. At first this imitation gave me no advantage, but after several weeks I realized I was becoming far more attuned to the environment we moved through. I heard more, for one thing, and my senses now constantly alert, I occasionally saw a deer mouse or a grouse before they did. ... But I took from them the confidence to believe I could attune myself better to the woods by behaving as they did—minutely inspecting certain things, seeking vantage points, always sniffing at the air. I did, and felt vigorous, charged with alertness.

They moved always, it seemed one day, in search of clues. ...

—*Of Wolves and Men*

I think, as the twentieth century comes to a close, that we are coming to an understanding of animals different from the one that has guided us for the past three hundred years. We have begun to see again, as our primitive ancestors did, that animals are neither imperfect imitations of men nor machines that can be described entirely in terms of endocrine secretions and neutral impulses. Like us, they are genetically variable, and both the species and the individual are capable of unprecedented behavior. They are like us in the sense that we can figuratively talk of them as beings some of whose forms, movements, activities, and social organizations are analogous, but they are no more literally like us than are trees. To paraphrase Henry Beston, they move in another universe, as complete as we are, both of us caught at a moment in mid-evolution.

Of Wolves and Men

LORENZ, KONRAD Z. (1903–1989)
Austrian ethologist and author; winner of the Nobel Prize in physiology and medicine (1973)

Learning from Nature

A man can sit for hours before an aquarium and stare into it as into the flames of an open fire or the rushing waters of a torrent. All conscious thought is happily lost in this state of apparent vacancy, and yet, in these hours of idleness, one learns essential truths about the macrocosm and the microcosm. ...

—*King Solomon's Ring*

Strange what blind faith is placed in proverbs, even when what they say is false or mis-
leading. The fox is not more cunning than other
beasts of prey and is much more stupid than wolf
or dog, the dove is certainly not peaceful, and of
the fish, rumour spreads only untruth: it is
neither so cold-blooded as one says of dull
people, nor is the "fish in water" nearly so
happily situated as the converse saying ["as
unhappy as a fish out of water"] would imply.
—*King Solomon's Ring*

Animal Proverbs Without Truth

... the act of killing in a beast of prey is
entirely free from hatred. It is self-evident and
yet paradoxical that the beast of prey bears no
more resentment towards the animal it intends
to kill than I do towards the boiled ham which I
intend to eat for supper and whose delicious
odor emanating from the kitchen presages a
pleasant evening. ...
—*Man Meets Dog*

The Predator: Free from Hate

The fidelity of a dog is a precious gift
demanding no less binding moral responsibilities
than the friendship of a human being. The bond
with a true dog is as lasting as the ties of this
earth can ever be, a fact which should be noted
by anyone who decides to acquire a canine
friend. ...
—*Man Meets Dog*

Man and Dog—Our Moral Responsibility

... One must never expect a wild animal to
treat a human being differently from a member of
its own species. ...
—*Man Meets Dog*

Impartiality

Our Love for Animals

    ... Only that kind of love for animals is beautiful and edifying which arises from the broader and more general love of the whole world of living creatures, a love whose most important and central feature must always be the love of mankind. ...

—*Man Meets Dog*

LUCRETIUS (98?–55 B.C.)
(TITUS LUCRETIUS CARUS)
Roman poet

Unto All, Their Seasons

    ... we behold each thing soever renewed,
And unto all, their seasons, after their kind,
Wherein they arrive the flower of their age.

—*Of the Nature of Things*

The Seasons of the Sky

We view the constellations of the night;
And that with us, the seasons of the sky
They thus, alternately divide ...

—*Of the Nature of Things*

Life Out of Death

    ... Nature ever
Upbuilds one thing from other, suffering naught
To come to birth but through some
        other's death.

—*Of the Nature of Things*

Limitations

    ... nature hath inviolably decreed,
What each can do, what each can never do ...

—*Of the Nature of Things*

MACLEOD, FIONA (1855–1905)
(PEN NAME FOR WILLIAM SHARP)
English writer

In Winter Woods

Where the forest murmurs there is music: ancient, everlasting. Go to the winter woods: listen there, look, watch, and the "dead months" will give you a subtler secret than any you have yet found in the forest.

—*Where the Forest Murmurs*

MAETERLINCK, MAURICE (1862–1949)
Belgian poet, dramatist and essayist; winner of the Nobel Prize for literature (1911)

*The Honey Bee Man—
The Master of the Bees*

Man truly became the master of the bees, although furtively, and without their knowledge; directing all things without giving an order, receiving obedience but not recognition. For the destiny once imposed by the seasons he has substituted his will. He repairs the injustice of the year, unites hostile republics, and equalises wealth. He restricts or augments the births, regulates the fecundity of the queen, dethrones her and installs another in her place. ... He will, five or six times in succession deprive the bees of the fruit of their labour, without harming them, without their becoming discouraged or even impoverished. He proportions the store–houses and granaries of their dwellings to the harvest of flowers that the spring is spreading over the dip of the hills. In a word he does with them what he will, he obtains what he will, provided always that what he seeks be in accordance with their laws and virtues; ...

—*The Life of the Bee*

The Sting of the Bee

A legend of menace and peril still clings to the bees. There is the distressful recollection of her sting, which produces a pain so characteristic that one knows not wherewith to compare it; a kind of destroying dryness, a flame of the desert rushing over the wounded limb, as though these daughters of the sun had distilled a dazzling poison from their father's angry rays. ...

—_The Life of the Bee_

MARCUS AURELIUS (121–180 A.D.)
Roman emperor devoted to stoic philosophy

Nature Loves Change

Observe always that everything is the result of change, and get used to thinking that there is nothing Nature loves so well as to change existing forms and to make new ones like them.

—_Meditations_

MATTHIESSEN, PETER (1927–   )
One of the most distinguished nature writers in America; novelist, explorer and member of expeditions to Alaska, Northwest Territories, Peru, Nepal, East Africa and New Guinea; winner of the African Wildlife Leadership Foundation Award and the John Burroughs Medal (1982) for _Sand Rivers_

Dying in the Wild

Few wild creatures perish of old age. Sooner or later, in the wild, some combination of inherent weakness, injury, disease, parasites, or competition, or migration barriers, or ... weather ... will cause the wind bird to fall to the hawk or storm that in its years of strength it had outflown.

—_The Wind Birds_

The restlessness of shorebirds, their kinship with the distance and swift seasons, the wistful signal of their voices down the long coastlines of the world makes them, for me, the most affecting of wild creatures. I think of them as birds of wind, as "wind birds."

The voice of the black-bellied plover carries far, a fluting, melancholy *toor-a-lee*, or *pee-ur-ee* like a sea bluebird's, often heard before the bird is seen. In time of storm, it sometimes seems to be the only bird aloft for with its wing span of two feet or more, the black-bellied plover is a strong flier; circumpolar and almost cosmopolitan, it migrates down across the world from breeding grounds within the Arctic Circle. The sanderling is the white sandpiper or "peep" of summer beaches, the tireless toy bird that runs before the surf. ... the one sandpiper that most people have noticed. Yet how few notice it at all, and few of the fewer still who recognize it will ever ask themselves why it is there or where it might be going. We stand there heedless of an extraordinary accomplishment: the diminutive creature making way for us along the beaches of July may be returning from an annual spring voyage which took it from central Chile to nesting grounds in northeast Greenland, a distance of eight thousand miles. One has only to consider the life force packed tight into that puff of feathers to lay the mind wide open to the mysteries—the order of things, the why and the beginning. As we contemplate that sanderling, there by the shining sea, one question leads inevitably to another, and all questions come full circle to the questioner, paused momentarily in his own journey under the sun and sky.

—*The Wind Birds*

Departure of the Curlew

The departure of curlew from a given place often occurs just prior to a storm, and in ancient days, in England, the curlew's cry, the plover's whistle boded no man any good. In North England, curlews and whimbrels were called "Gabriel's hounds;" the name whimbrel comes from "whimpernel," ... attributed to it of houndlike whimperings. Both birds were known as harbingers of death, and in the sense that they are birds of passage, that in the wild melodies of their calls, in the breath of vast distance and bare regions that attends them, we sense intimations of our own mortality, there is justice in the legend. Yet it is not the death sign that the curlews bring, but only the memory of life, of a high beauty passing swiftly, as the curlew passes, leaving us in solitude on an empty beach, with summer gone, and a wind blowing.

—*The Wind Birds*

Battle of the Hippos

Despite appearances, hippos are sensitive and easily upset; they were not reconciled even hours later to the presence of Hugo's car, ... I noticed, however, that when real fights occurred between two males, the herd did not join in the uproar but fell silent, as if watching carefully for a sign that the hippo hierarchy was about to change. Even the Egyptian geese retired as the gigantic creatures reared up on their hind legs, mouths wide and ivory clacking, their huge heads locked, the titans twisted, crashing back into the water. ... Only when the fight was over did the nervous herd release its tensions, with a mighty uproar, as if the opinions of each one had been vindicated, subsiding shortly again as if nothing had happened.

—*Sand Rivers*

Killers at Work

Not far from camp, in the full heat of the day, five wild dogs were engaged in a wart-hog kill, yanking and tearing at the dying creature in an open grove of small yellowthorn acacia. In the dust and sun and yellow light, among skeletal small trees, the dogs in silhouette spun round and round the pig in a macabre dance in which the victim, although dead, seemed to take part. But within a few minutes, the wild pig had been rended for the dogs work fast perhaps to avoid sharing their prey with hyena or lion. The strange patched animals loped away into the woods, lugging ... gobbets of fresh pig meat in the direction of their den, returning soon to fetch away the last wet scraps, gray now and breaded with dust in the hard, hot wind.

"There's nature in the raw for you!" Melva exclaimed, as unsettled as all of us by the strange scene.

—*Sand Rivers*

The Wildebeest

The wildebeest has a goat's beard and a lion's mane and a slanty back like a hyena, the head is too big and the tail too long for this rickety thing, and Africans say that the wildebeest is a collection of the parts that were left over after God had finished up all other creatures.

—*Sand Rivers*

Walking Without Talking

Talking almost invariably detracts from the real pleasure of walking, in which one finally enters the surroundings. And in the wilderness the human voice is disturbing to animals we might otherwise see. ...

—*Sand Rivers*

The Missing Animals of September

Apart from this buffalo and a few small groups of elephant, animals in this long-grass country have been scarce, as if all the waning energy in the coppered hills and yellowed trees and sinking rivers of September had been distilled in the fierce greens of the parrots and paradisal blues of the brilliant rollers. But on the far side of a rise, in an open hollow, the missing animals have taken shelter from the silent landscape—impala, wildebeest, wart hog, zebra, and elephant with a flock of huge *batutu* in attendance. Led by the hornbills, all but the elephant stream away uphill toward the blue sky, striped horses shining in the high bronze grass.

—*Sand Rivers*

MILLS, ENOS ABIJAH (1870–1922)
Naturalist, author, conservationist and friend of John Muir

Of all the birds of the Rockies, the one most marvelously eloquent is the solitaire. I have often felt that everything stood still and that every beast and bird listened while the matchless solitaire sang. The hermit thrush seems to suppress one, to give one a touch of reflective loneliness; but the solitaire stirs one to be up and doing, gives one the spirit of youth. In the solitaire's song one feels all the freshness and the promise of spring. I was camping alone one evening in the deep solitude of the Rockies. The slanting sun-rays were glowing on St. Vrain's crag-crowned hills ... when from a near-by treetop came the triumphant, hopeful song of a solitaire. ... One believes in fairies when the solitaire sings. Some of my friends have predicted that I shall some time meet with an accident and perish in the solitudes alone. If their prediction should come true, I shall hope it will be in the summer ... and that during my last conscious moments I shall hear the melody of the solitaire singing.

—*Wildlife on the Rockies*

Song of the Solitaire

MILNE, LORUS J. (1910–) AND **MARGERY** (1915–)
University professors (husband and wife),
exploring scientists, photographers, lecturers
and winners of many science writing awards

Explaining Nature

Generally we try to oversimplify nature. We
expect one explanation to suffice, as a sort of
universal truth. If a pigeon, a shearwater and a
salmon use cues from the sun in their direc-
tional sense, we look for this same system in all
other kinds of life able to migrate or to find the
way home. Yet landmarks are highly important
to some animals, as they are also to us. Possibly
an abalone snail uses some underwater equivalent of landmarks when it leaves its daytime
resting spot to feed elsewhere in darkness, only
to return before dawn to its homesite. At
present, we lack information on the naviga-
tional aids important to various kinds of animals. But almost certainly they include nearly
every sensory stimulus to which life responds.

—*The Senses of Animals and Men*

We suspect that the scientist and the poet have more in common than either of them ordinarily admits. The sense of wonder reaches both. We believe it was the sense Dame Edith Sitwell had in mind when she wrote of any good poet that "Like Moses, he sees God in the burning bush when the half-opened or myopic physical eye sees only the gardener burning leaves." The sense of wonder seems to slip over a special part of a person's self, and to fit so well that the world thereafter seems different, more pleasing, more important. The lure of the unknown grows clearer, ever irresistible.

—*The Senses of Animals and Men*

... Change in cultural directions, rather than in physical ones, has been the mode of progress in human evolution. Admittedly we live longer than our ancestors. We grow taller, have bigger feet and tend to lose our "wisdom teeth" because of changes in environment and habits, such as diet. But will our sense organs, like our wisdom teeth, atrophy if we use them less and less in cultured communities? We've never solved the riddle as to whether blind cave animals lost their eyes from lack of use after generations in the dark, or are the descendants from blind creatures that blundered into caves and survived only in complete darkness. Are we engineering adventures out of life? Adventures are what we need our senses for. Our savage ancestors depended on their senses every hour of every day. ...

—*The Senses of Animals and Men*

MOMADAY, N. SCOTT (1934–)

Native American (Kiowa) from Oklahoma; winner of the Pulitzer Prize (1969) for his first novel, *House Made of Dawn*; prose and poetry writer; teacher of English at the University of California; professor of English at Stanford University; teacher in English Department at the University of Arizona; author of *The Way to Rainy Mountain* (1969)

Sounds

The land settles into the end of summer. In the white light a whirlwind moves far out in the plain, and afterwards there is something like a shadow on the grass, a tremor, nothing. There seems a stillness at noon, but that is illusion: the landscape rises and falls, ringing. In the dense growth of the bottomland a dark drift moves on the Washita River. A spider enters a small pool of light on Rainy Mountain Creek, and downstream at the convergence, a Channel catfish turns around in the current and slithers to the surface, where a dragonfly hovers and darts. Away on the high ground grasshoppers and bees set up a crackle and roar in the fields, and meadowlarks and scissortails whistle and wheel about. Somewhere in a maze of gullies a calf shivers and bawls in a tangle of chinaberry trees. And high in the distance a hawk turns in the sun and sails. ...

—*Words in the Blood: Contemporary Indian Writers of North and South America*

MONTAIGNE, MICHEL DE (1533–1592)
French moralist and creator of the personal
essay

I quote others only to better express myself.
—*The Essays of Michel de Montaigne*

Quoting Others

I care not so much what I am in another's
judgement, as I care what I am in my own. I
wish to be rich of myself, not by borrowing.
—*The Essays of Michel de Montaigne*

*To Thine Ownself
Be True*

… Miracles exist from our ignorance of
nature, not in nature herself.
—*The Essays of Michel de Montaigne*

*The Miraculous
in Nature*

I hold that what can not be accomplished
by reasoning and by discretion and skill is never
accomplished by force. I was thus brought up.
—*The Essays of Michel de Montaigne*

Reasoning or Force

My profession and my art is living. Whoever
forbids me speak of this according to my percep-
tions, experience, and habits, let him bid the
architect talk about buildings, not according to
his own ideas, but according to those of his
neighbor; according to another's knowledge, not
according to his own.
—*The Essays of Michel de Montaigne*

Self-Truths

Even if I could make myself feared, I should
still prefer to make myself loved.
—*The Essays of Michel de Montaigne*

The Quality of Love

Poetic License

One can play the fool everywhere else, but not in poetry.

'Mediocrity in poets is not permitted by the gods nor by men ...

... there is nothing more confident than a bad poet.'

—*The Essays of Michel de Montaigne*

MUIR, JOHN (1838–1914)
Scottish-born American naturalist, writer and wilderness conservationist

The Voice of Mountain Waters

There is nothing more eloquent in Nature than a mountain stream.

—*A Thousand Mile Walk to the Gulf*

Mysteries in Winds

We know ... little of winds ... despite the powers of science. ... the substance of the winds is too thin for human eyes, their written language is too difficult for human minds, and their spoken language mostly too faint for the ears.

—*A Thousand Mile Walk to the Gulf*

The Stay-At-Home Streams of Florida

Most streams appear to travel through a country with thoughts and plans for something beyond. But those of Florida ... do not appear to be traveling at all, and seem to know nothing of the sea.

—*A Thousand Mile Walk to the Gulf*

The Immortality of Plants

They tell us that plants are perishable, soulless creatures, that only man is immortal, but this, I think, is something that we know very nearly nothing about.

—*A Thousand Mile Walk to the Gulf*

I have seen oaks of many species in many kinds of exposure and soil, but those of Kentucky excel in grandeur all I had ever before beheld. They are broad and dense and bright green. In the leafy bowers and caves of their long branches dwell magnificent avenues of shade, and every tree seems to be blessed with a double portion of strong, exulting life.

—*A Thousand Mile Walk to the Gulf*

The Grandeur of Oaks in Kentucky

On no subject are our ideas more warped and pitiable than on death. Instead of the sympathy, the friendly union, of life and death so apparent in Nature, we are taught that death is an accident, a deplorable punishment for the oldest sin. ... But let children walk with Nature ... and they will learn that death is stingless indeed, and as beautiful as life, and that the grave has no victory, for it never fights.

—*A Thousand Mile Walk to the Gulf*

Fear of Death

MURPHY, ROBERT CUSHMAN (1887–1973)
Curator of ornithology, naturalist, writer and explorer; winner of the John Burroughs Medal for *Oceanic Birds of South America* (1938)

No being can reveal more marvelous grace than a whale. Do not think of them as shapeless, as I once did, because of seeing only bloated carcasses washed ashore on Long Island beaches. ... Envision this magnificent blue whale, as shapely as a mackerel, spending the last ounce of strength and life in a hopeless contest against cool, unmoved, insensate man.

—*Logbook for Grace*

The Grace of a Living Whale

The Magical World of Children

OLSON, SIGURD F. (1899–1982)
Author, naturalist, ecologist, wilderness guide and preservationist, geologist, university dean and professor; winner of the John Burroughs Medal for *Wilderness Days* (1974)

Children live in a world not only of their own, but peopled with all they imagine. Their lives are rich and colored because of it, just as those of adults are enriched by their knowledge of all that has gone before. But the young have a special faculty of listening and understanding and are conscious of the unseen. During my early years I instinctively sought out places where the feelings were strong. One place I came to know long after the days of the nest in the alder swamp was a great pine near the shore of a lake. I used to curl up there on a bed of pine needles between two roots; I was part of the pine and the pine of me, for I could feel it move in the wind

The Pipes no longer sound as often or as clearly as they once did, but I know they are there and that children still hear them. I can tell by the light in their eyes, the sudden catch in their voices, by the constant listening and awareness of things that may be lost to me.

—*Open Horizons*

In a canoe a man changes and the life he has lived seems strangely remote. Time is no longer of moment, for he has become part of space and freedom. What matters is that he is heading down the misty trail of explorers and *voyageurs*, with a fair wind and a chance for a good camp somewhere ahead. The future is other lakes, countless rapids and the sound of them, portages through muskeg and over the ledges.

A man is part of his canoe and therefore part of all it knows. The instant he dips a paddle, he flows as it flows, the canoe yielding to his slightest touch, responsive to his every whim and thought. The paddle is an extension of his arm, as his arm is part of his body. But to the canoeman there is nothing that compares with the joy he knows when a paddle is in his hand.

—*Wilderness Days*

Two years ago I walked out on the Sonoran desert at midnight with the stars so bright they seemed like planets close to earth. I had come to listen to the coyotes sing, smell the desert, and catch its feeling. On top of a hill I found a barren lodge from which I could look out across a valley and get a view of the heavens as well. Then began that strange haunting medley of blended notes I had come to hear, first only one, then several, until the night was alive with music. Suddenly they stopped, and it was the same as when listening to the loons of the Quetico-Superior—the stillness descended. ...

—*Open Horizons*

The Oneness of Man and Canoe

Coyotes, Loons and Silence

Passing of the Voyageurs

Not until I began guiding in the region the French *voyageurs* had traveled did I begin to sense its color and history. I came to know some of the descendants of these men, who gave me my first living picture of the past. ... When I paddled down the waterways, ran the rapids, and made the portages those old canoemen had trod, mine was a sense of personal identification. ... These gay French Canadian canoemen with red sashes and caps, singing in the face of monotony and disaster, were the ones who stood out.

But the gaudy brigades are gone now, no longer are retipped paddles flashing in the sun, no more the singing and the sound of voices across the water—nothing left but crumbling forts, old foundations, and the names they left behind them. There is something that will never be lost, however; the *voyageur* as a symbol of a way of life, the gay spirit with which he faced enormous odds, and a love of the wilderness few other frontiersmen ever knew.

—*Wilderness Days*

Joys of the Aware and Alive

Joys come from simple and natural things, mists over meadows, sunlight on leaves, the path of the moon over water. Even rain and wind and stormy clouds bring joy, just as knowing animals and flowers and where they live. Such things are where you find them, and belong to the aware and alive. They require little scientific knowledge, but bring in their train an ecological perspective, and a way of looking at the world.

—*Open Horizons*

Once I said that trout fishing is a spiritual thing, and after a lifetime, I know it is true. For that matter, all fishing is a spiritual thing to a boy, no matter what he catches. The sense of surprise, the eternal wonder of a fish coming out of the water, the deep inherent sense of primitive accomplishment in getting food by simple means, and the Pipes always playing softly in the background—no wonder all boys love fishing, no wonder all men, who are really boys at heart, feel the same.

—*Open Horizons*

Trout Fishing—
A Spiritual Thing

PATON, ALAN (1903–1988)
South African novelist and humanitarian worker

When you get older you do not feel the issues quite so deeply. You've learned the lesson that success is not the goal. Some things you've got to do for their own sake.

—*Interview with* New York Times
Correspondent,
Tertius Myburgh, December 23, 1969

Changing with Time

PEATTIE, DONALD CULROSS (1898–1964)
American author and botanist

How Audubon Lived

... he was a genius ... of art. ... But Audubon had, too, a genius for the art of living. He lived with zest for the adventure, and with personal ardors. He savored everything, even the unsavory. He saw almost everything, from 1803 to 1849, from Florida to Labrador, from New York City to Fort Union on the borders of Montana. He lived among Pennsylvania Quakers, in Kentucky among pioneers from Virginia, in New Orleans among Creoles, in Mississippi among planters, in North Dakota among Indians. He explored Maine and South Carolina, Texas and Florida. He knew all types; he was the friend of Daniel Boone and Daniel Webster. ...

—*Audubon's America*

The Ghostly Comet

But what, after all, is a comet? Nothing more ghostly exists in time or space; it rushes at us out of a black hole of space, trails a fire that does not burn, a light that is no light, and looping close to the sun, vanishes again into space—to return at the appointed time when the sea of darkness again gives up its dead; or, more terrible still, never to return from its Avernus.

—*An Almanac for Moderns*

As soon as the green and violet hour of summer dusk is at hand and the bats begin to sweep the sky for midges, the voice of the whippoorwill rises out of the hollow below my house. For it is a nostalgic and intensely American sound, and one that goes back, as we find nearly everything precious does, to childhood.

—An Almanac for Moderns

The Call of the Whippoorwill

It is natural that women should like the birds whose domestic affairs can be observed under the eaves; they love the sweetest singers, the brightest plumage, the species not too shy to be seen at close range. For them the waders and swimmers, the awkward of leg, the harsh of cry, the wild of soul have seldom the same appeal. But that which flees from men, that will men have. Women of all people ought to understand this, but they do not, quite.

—An Almanac for Moderns

Women and Birds

But the name of a bird is nothing but the opening of a door to knowledge; it is not knowledge in itself, and the pleasures of study consist in making one's self a Sherlock Holmes, intent upon every trace and detail of one's subject's life.

—An Almanac for Moderns

Bird Study

I am not ... certain that I want to be able to identify all the warblers. There is a charm sometimes in not knowing what or who the singer is.

—An Almanac for Moderns

A Charm in Not Knowing

Song of the White-throat

... the meadowlark is like the ... happy whistle of the wind through the grass ... and the thrush is the voice of serenity, of green twilights in very lonely hushed woods. ...But the white-throat's touching chromatic pierces the heart; it blends sadness and happiness. ... a song like a cry, a song that speaks of the antiquity of time, the briefness of life.

—*An Almanac for Moderns*

The Time to Hear Bird Music

The time to hear bird music is between four and six in the morning. Seven o'clock is not too late, but by eight the fine rapture is over, due, I suspect, to the contentment of the inner man that comes with breakfast; a poet should always be hungry or have a lost love.

—*An Almanac for Moderns*

Identifying Birds

Flowers are best identified ... by one's self. But with the birds, a guide ... to point out what you ought to have seen, to pass you the binoculars and whisper eagerly in your ear, is worth a shelf of books.

—*An Almanac for Moderns*

To Possess Nature

A man need not know how to name all the oaks or the moths, or be able to recognize a synclinal fault, or tell time by the stars, in order to possess Nature. He may have his mind solely on growing larkspurs, or he may love a boat and a sail and a blue-eyed day at sea. He may have a bent for making paths or banding birds, or he may be only an inveterate and curious walker.

—*An Almanac for Moderns*

All through commonplace observation of
Nature runs an infatuation with the rare that is
the mark of limited understanding ... the
veteran student knows that rarity is chiefly one
of the illusions of the provincial point of view.
    —*An Almanac for Moderns*

Infatuation with Rarity

A man's real religion is that about which he
becomes excited, the object or the cause he will
defend, the point at which, spontaneously, he
cries out in joy over a victory, or groans aloud
from an injury.
    —*An Almanac for Moderns*

A Man's Real Religion

The purpose of studying Nature at all, aside
from the distraction which it affords ... is that
the study should illuminate the relation of living
things to each other, to us, to the environment.
One thing *should* lead to something quite other.
The goal of biological thought is ramification,
many-view-pointedness, and a man who drops
his swallows uncompleted because he has
suddenly grown excited over beetles is simply a
man who is growing.
    —*An Almanac for Moderns*

*The Purpose of
Studying Nature*

The harvest moon has no innocence, like
the slim quarter moon of a spring twilight, nor
has it the silver penny brilliance of the moon
that looks down upon the resorts of summer
time. Wise, ripe, and portly, like an old
Bacchus, it waxes night after night.
    —*An Almanac for Moderns*

The Waxing Moon

Requisite for a Wood Fire

There is but one requisite of a fire, that it should burn. For myself I like best to woo it with pine, both as kindling and logwood. Pine burns brighter and hotter, and needs less kindling than any other wood. It has the sweetest odor and sizzles contentedly. What good is a cat that does not purr, a chestnut that will not pop, or a log that can not sing?

—*An Almanac for Moderns*

Man's Hostility to Nature

All about me I am presented with a people, blood of my blood and dear to me, who have no capacity to enjoy that which they have. In place of the forest turned to account without injury ... my neighbors who burn off the woods every year from sheer incompetence to enjoy their blessings, from an innate hostility to Nature.

—*An Almanac for Moderns*

Beauty— The Truth of Things

Beauty, great beauty, is for me the fitting of the object to its use, the truth of things.

—*An Almanac for Moderns*

Winter Days Afield

The true lover of nature does not complain of his mistress that now she turns a colder cheek. He takes his luck abroad like the small birds that all through the leafless woods scurry in little gusts before him.

—*An Almanac for Moderns*

Animal Trails

The moment when a fresh fall of snow is on the ground is the opportunity for finding out what your animal neighbors do with themselves and where they go.

—*An Almanac for Moderns*

Now in the south, these nights, rides Scorpio, the very spirit of the hot month of July. The head and the crablike pincers turn westward. In the center of the long body glows the brilliant red star, Antares. ... The body trails away to the long tail, then rests on the southern horizon, the stars composing it being rather faint where they cross the Milky Way, but coming out stronger at the tail itself, where it is erect and flung forward as if the scorpion were preparing to sting.

Scorpio—
The Spirit of July

—An Almanac for Moderns

There is no philosophy with a shadow of realism about it, save a philosophy based upon Nature.

Philosophy and Nature

—An Almanac for Moderns

They are never to be forgotten—that first bird pursued through thicket ... not to kill but to know it, or that first plant lifted reverently and excitedly about the earth. No spring returns but that I wish I might live again through the moment when I went out in the woods ... to learn not only the name, but the ways and the range and the charm of the windflower.

Thrill of First Discovery

—An Almanac for Moderns

Night terrors are bred in closets, beds, cellars, attics, and all those traps and pits and sinks in which civilized man houses himself. ... Out in the open night it may be cold, or windy, or rainy, but it is never anything in which a bogy could endure.

Night Terrors

—An Almanac for Moderns

The Loveliness of Vanishing Things

Nothing in this world is really precious until we know that it will soon be gone. The lily, the starry daffodil, the regal iris ... are the lovelier for their imminent vanishing. The snow crystal has but touched earth ere it begins to die.

—An Almanac for Moderns

Cricket Song

I love to hear the crickets chanting when I drop toward sleep. ... They sing, I think, of orange moons and meadow mice, of the first hoar frost lying pure and cool ... and of the falling of ... gold globes from the persimmon tree. ...

—An Almanac for Moderns

The Fateful Moth

If the word butterfly connotes something fair and frail, a creature of the sunlight hour, so when we pronounce the name of a moth we think of something fateful—a creature that will fling itself upon a candle flame to die, a thief of time that, working in the dark in the blazing heat of attics where we never venture now, corrupts as surely as time and rust. Every association of moths is with night and mystery and death.

—An Almanac for Moderns

The Pitch Pine

I like our loblolly pines for their long glittering foliage full of warmth and light at all seasons, bringing back to me the very smell of the South. ... I like the yellow pine for its generous armored trunks. ... But it is the pitch pine that you have all that was ever embodied in the name of pine. ...

—An Almanac for Moderns

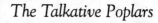

The wise of the earth assure us that all poplars, like the willows, are trivial trees, short of life, weak of stem, prey to more ills than mortal man. These things are so, and we are bidden only to admire the oak and pine, that outlive the centuries. ... But is there no room in the forest for the poplar, with its restless talkative foliage? The strong and silent folk of earth—I would rather praise them than live with them. I have never grumbled at a chatterbox, providing that her tongue was kind.

The Talkative Poplars

—*An Almanac for Moderns*

A tree in its old age is like a bent but mellowed and wise old man; it inspires our respect and tender admiration; it is too noble to need our pity.

Old Trees

—*An Almanac for Moderns*

Summer flowers distract us with well upon a hundred families ... autumn flowers are ... almost wholly ... the tall rank composites. But something in the spring flora, perfect in its simplicity and unity, carries us back to Arcady.

Simplicity of Spring Flowers

—*An Almanac for Moderns*

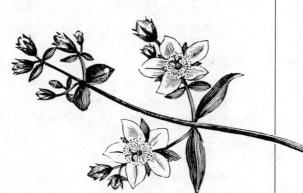

PETERSON, ROGER TORY (1908–)
Ornithologist, bird artist, author and originator
of the famous Peterson Nature Guides; winner
of the John Burroughs Medal for *Birds Over
America* (1950)

*The "Unrestrained"
Birds and a Confession*

A bird can fly where it wants to when it
wants to. I am sure that is what appealed to me
when I was in school. Regimentation and
restriction rubbed me the wrong way; and the
boys in my neighborhood were either younger or
older, so I had to dream up my own fun. There
were times when I wished that I could fly as
they did and leave everything.

As I learned more about birds I found they
are not quite the gloriously unrestrained things I
had imagined them to be. They are bound by all
sorts of natural laws. They go north and south
almost by the calendar. They seem to follow
certain flyways and routes between their summer and winter homes. A robin that lives in
Connecticut this year will not think of going to
Wisconsin next year. A night heron newly
arrived in the rookery goes through a step-by-
step ritual of song and dance. Leave out any one
of the steps, and the sequence is disrupted—the
reproductive cycle does not carry through.

I learned, too, that most birds have "territory." They are property owners just as we are—
and song, instead of being only a joyous out-
burst, is a functional expression—a proclama-
tion of ownership, an invitation to a female, a
threat to another male.

Birds then, are almost as earth-bound as we
are. They have freedom and mobility only
within prescribed limits. ... But my interest

survived this phase and has grown deeper. What had started as an emotional release has swung over to an intellectual pursuit.

Reluctant at first to accept the strait jacket of a world which I did not comprehend, I finally, with the help of my hobby, made some sort of peace with society. The birds, which started as an escape from the unreal, bridged the gap to reality and became a key whereby I might unlock eternal things.

—*Birds Over America*

RICKETT, HAROLD WILLIAM (1896–)
American author of books about wildflowers,
editor of *The Wildflowers of the United States*
(multivolume series) and staff member of the
New York Botanical Gardens

Two Kinds of Men

Of the many kinds of men who go to and fro
on the earth, we may notice two: those whose
passion it is to describe things; and those who
inquire also into the causes.

—*The Green Earth*

Illusion

One of the common pastimes of the natural
scientist is thus exemplified: to propound that
what looks like a leaf is not a leaf, what looks
like a seed is not a seed, what looks like a bug is
not a bug,—in general that things are not what
they seem.

—*The Green Earth*

The Poet of the Soil

I know a man who is a poet. It is true that
he would not know himself by such a title, for
he does not write verse; he is a farmer. He is a
poet because he knows the joy of creation. A
never-failing delight is the appearance of
living, growing plants in a patch of dirt where,
only a few days before, he has placed some dry
grains. ...

—*The Green Earth*

ROOSEVELT, THEODORE (1858–1919)

Twenty-sixth president of the United States, outstanding field naturalist, explorer, conservationist, authority on big game animals and birder

Advice for an Adventurer

The man should have youth and strength who seeks adventure in the wide, waste spaces of the earth, in the marshes, and among the vast mountain masses, in the northern forests, amid the steaming jungles of the tropics, or on the deserts of sand or of snow. He must long greatly for the lonely winds that blow across the wilderness, and for sunrise and sunset over the rim of the empty world. His heart must thrill for the saddle and not the hearthstone. He must be helmsman and chief, the cragsman, the rifleman, the boat steerer. He must be the wielder of axe and of paddle, the rider of fiery horses, the master of the craft that leaps through white waters. His eye must be true and quick, his hand steady and strong. His heart must never fail nor his head grow bewildered, whether he faces brute and human foes, or the frowning strength of hostile nature, or the awful fear that grips those who are lost in trackless lands. Wearing toil and hardship shall be his; thirst and famine he shall face, and burning fever. Death shall come to greet him with poison-fang or poison-arrow, in ... charging beast or of scaly things that lurk in lake and river; it shall lie in wait for him among untrodden forests, in the swirl of wild waters, and in the blast of snow blizzard of thunder-shattered hurricane.

—*A Book-Lover's Holidays in the Open*

RUSKIN, JOHN (1819–1900)

English writer and critic, stylist, lecturer and social and economic reformist

Solemnity of Dawn

There is no solemnity so deep, to a rightly thinking creature, as that of dawn.

SA'DI (1184–1291)
(PEN NAME OF MUSHARRIF-UDDIN)

A Persian poet; perhaps the most popular of all time

The Lucky and the Unlucky

Property is for the comfort of life, not for the accumulation of wealth. A sage, having been asked who is lucky and who is not replied: "He is lucky who has eaten and sowed, but he is unlucky who has died and not enjoyed."

—*Tales from the Gulistan*

Kindness

Who desires succour in the day of calamity says to him: "Be generous in the times of prosperity." The slave with a ring in his ear, if not cherished, will depart. Be kind, because then a stranger will become thy slave.

—*Tales from the Gulistan*

Patience and Wisdom

Who has no patience, has no wisdom.

—*Tales from the Gulistan*

Friends and Enemies

Confide not to thy friend every secret thou possessest; how knoweth thou that he will not some time become thy foe? Inflict not every injury thou canst upon an enemy, because it is possible that one day he may become thy friend.

—*Tales from the Gulistan*

SASS, HERBERT RAVENEL (1884–1958)
American nature writer and southern
author

Nature—wild Nature—dwells in gardens
just as she dwells in the tangled woods, in the
deeps of the sea, and on the heights of the
mountains; and the wilder the garden, the more
you will see of her there. If you would see her
unspoiled and in many forms, let your garden be
a wild place, a place of trees and shrubs and
vines and grass, even a place where weeds are
granted a certain tolerance; for gardens which
are merely spick and span plots of combed and
curried flower-beds have little attraction for the
birds or for the other people of the wild. Yet,
into any garden, no matter how artificial or how
tame, some wild things will find their way. It is a
shallow boast, this talk that we hear about man's
conquest of nature. It will be time to talk in that
fashion when man has learned to check or
control the march of the seasons or when he has
brought some spot of earth so thoroughly under
his dominion that it remains insensible to the
impulse of the spring. He has not done that yet,
and he never will. Spring in a garden is as
irresistible, as incredible, as spring in the heart
of the wilderness.

—*Adventures in Green Places*

The Wild Garden

The Colossal Calamity—Extinction

No poem, no painting, no work of man's hand or brain is as marvellous a thing as the least of the species of living beings that inhabit the earth. Each one ... is a miracle as far beyond our comprehension as the stars. We cannot make them, we cannot understand how they were made. To destroy one ... to wipe out a whole species ... for all eternity, is to do so colossal a thing that the mind falters at the thought. Yet we have done it again and again and again, thoughtlessly, needlessly, wantonly, cruelly ... many of the species that we have destroyed—or are now destroying—were among the noblest and most beautiful.

—*On the Wings of a Bird*

SCHOPENHAUER, ARTHUR (1788–1860)
German philosopher

The Pleasure We Get from Work

There is a direct pleasure in seeing work grow under one's hands day by day, until at last it is finished. This is the pleasure attaching to a work of art or a manuscript or even mere manual labor; and, of course, the higher the work, the greater pleasure it will give us.

—*The Complete Essays*

The Value of Self-Control

Nothing will protect us from external compulsion so much as the control of ourselves; and as Seneca says, to submit yourself to reason is the way to make everything else submit to you.

—*The Complete Essays*

The sight of any free animal going about its business undisturbed, seeking its food, or looking after its young, or mixing in the company of its kind, all the time being exactly what it ought to be and can be,—what a strange pleasure it gives us! Even if it is only a bird, I can watch it for a long time with delight; or a water rat or a hedgehog; or better still a weasel, a deer or a stag. The main reason why we take so much pleasure in looking at animals is that we like to see our own nature in such a simplified form. There is only one mendacious being in the world, and that is man. Every other is true and sincere, and makes no attempt to conceal what it is, expressing its feelings just as they are.

—*From an Essay,*
"Psychological Observations"

Why We Delight in Watching Animals

SCHWEITZER, ALBERT (1875–1965)
Alsatian philosopher, humanist, musician, theologian, missionary and expounder of ethical system "Reverence for Life"

We must never permit the voice of humanity within us to be silenced. It is man's sympathy with all creatures that first makes him truly a man.

—*The Animal World of Albert Schweitzer*

Never Silence the Voice of Humanity

A Prayer for Animals

When Albert Schweitzer was a child, before he began going to school, it was quite incomprehensible to him that in his evening prayers, he should be expected to pray only for human beings. ...

"So when my mother had prayed with me and had kissed me good-night, I used to add silently a prayer that I had composed myself for all living creatures. It ran thus:

'Oh Heavenly Father, protect and bless all things that have breath; guard them from all evil and let them sleep in peace.'"

—*The Animal World of Albert Schweitzer*

SCOTT, ROBERT FALCON (1868–1912)
English Antarctic explorer, naval officer, bird painter and writer who died on an expedition to the South Pole; father of Peter Scott, English ornithologist

Nature Games

Teach the boy nature study, it is better than games.

—*From his diary*

SEARS, PAUL BIGELOW (1891–)
American botanist, teacher, conservationist, ecologist and author

Conservation

Conservation is a way of living and an attitude that humanity must adopt if it wants to live decently and permanently on earth.

—*Conservation, Please*

SHAKESPEARE, WILLIAM (1564–1616)
English poet, playwright and actor

And the poor beetle, that we tread upon,
In corporal sufferance finds a pang as great
As when a giant dies.
>   —*Measure for Measure, Act III*

The Poor Beetle

In Nature's Infinite book of secrecy
A little I can read.
>   —*Antony and Cleopatra,*
>   *Act I, Scene II*

Reading Nature

SHAPLEY, HARLOW (1885–1972)
American astronomer, professor of astronomy,
Harvard University and director of Harvard
Observatory

I like these men of understanding who play
Boswell to the specialist. They often have a gift
greater than that of the concentrated workers
whom they soften up for us. For they have
breadth and perspective, which help us to get at
the essence of a problem more objectively than
we could even if we were fully equipped with
the language and knowledge of the fact-bent
explorer and analyst. The scientific interpreters
frequently enhance our enjoyment in that they
give us of themselves, as well as of the discoverers whose exploits they recount. We are always
grateful to them, moreover, for having spared us
labor and possibly discouragement.
>   —*A Treasury of Science*

*Salute to the
Science-Writers*

The Mark of the Scientist

One quality which sets the scientist apart is the persistence of his curiosity about the world. ... he may spend months or even years on some quest, seemingly trivial yet destined perhaps to prove a clue to the origin of a race. Or ... he may spend countless hours beside a murky pond, waiting for a turtle to lay her eggs. ... In both ... there is much of the excitement, the emotional and intellectual spirit of the scientific quest.

—*A Treasury of Science*

SHARP, DALLAS LORE (1870–1929)
American author, naturalist and educator

To Kill Will Spoil the Day

A rusty, red-bellied water-snake, in a mat of briers nearby, relaxed and straightened slowly out,—and softly, that I might not be attracted,—stretched himself to the warmth. I could have broken his back with my paddle. ... But to strike him asleep in the sun simply because he was a snake would have robbed the spot of part of its life and spirit and robbed me of serenity for the rest of the day. I should not have been able to enjoy the quiet again until I had said my prayers and slept.

—*Roof and Meadow*

There must be a dragon in the way, I suppose—in the way even of nature study. There are unpleasant, perhaps unnecessary, and evil creatures —snakes!—in the fields and woods, which we must be willing to meet and tolerate for the love within us. Tick-seeds, beggar-needles, mud, mosquitoes, rain, heat, hawks and snakes haunt all our paths, hindering us sometimes, though never really blocking the way.

—*Roof and Meadow*

He is college bred. He observes nature "scientifically," he says. He knows what he knows, namely, that *Coccinella septempunctata* is *septempunctata*, and not *novemnotata*. All he knows (and what else is there to know?) is *septempunctata* and *novemnotata*—the names of things, the places, parts, laws, and theories of things. He is the text-book naturalist.

We have been afield together a few times, but I was never able to interest or surprise him, because there were no surprises left: he knew everything. He had dissected every flower, measured every bird, stuck a pin through every butterfly; he had a glacial theory for every pebble, a chemical theory for every glow-worm, and a pile of science for the color of the autumn leaves. ... He had memorized *Coccinella septempunctata*, but he did not know the lady bird.

—*Roof and Meadow*

Nature's Dragons

The Textbook Naturalist

Nature's True Lover

Poetry is not in birds and sunsets and moonlight,—not in things,—but like the kingdom of heaven and other things divine, it is in us, in ourselves. It is a mistake to go about ... sticking poems, the poet's poems, over earth and sea and sky, imagining that this is loving nature, that this is knowing the out-of-doors.

How shall we see mice in the grass or hear toads in the puddles with our heads cloud-wreathed and our spirits afloat in the ether beyond the stars?

—Roof and Meadow

Our Hungry Crows

There are few of our winter birds that go hungry so often as do ... the crows, and that die in so great numbers for lack of food and shelter.

After severe and protracted cold, with a snow-covered ground, a crow-roost looks like a battlefield, so thick lie the dead and wounded. Morning after morning the flock goes over to forage in the frozen fields, and night after night returns hungrier, weaker, and less able to resist the cold. Now, as the darkness falls, a bitter wind breaks loose and sweeps down upon the pines and how often I have thought me of the crows biding the night yonder in the moaning pines. So often, as a boy, and with so real an awe, I have watched them returning at night, that the crows will never cease flying through my wintry sky,—an endless line of wavering black figures, weary, retreating figures, beating over in the early dusk.

—Winter

The snow had melted away from the river meadows. ... I had stopped beside a tiny bundle of bones that lay in the matted grass. ...

I had recognized the bones at once as the skeleton of a muskrat. But it was something peculiar in the way they lay that had caused me to pause. They seemed outstretched, as if composed by gentle hands, the hands of sleep. The delicate ribs had fallen in, but not a bone was broken or displaced, not one showed the splinter of shot, or the crack that might have been made by a steel trap. No violence had been done them. They had been touched by nothing rougher than the snow. Out into the hidden runway they had crept. Death had passed by them here; but no one else in all the winter.

The creature had died—a "natural" death. It had starved while a hundred acres of plenty lay round about. Picking up the skull, I found the jaws locked together as if they were a single solid bone. One of the two incisor teeth of the

Death of a Muskrat—
Malocclusion

upper jaw was missing, and apparently had never developed. The opposite tooth on the lower jaw, thus unopposed and so unworn, had grown beyond its normal height up into the empty socket above, then on, turning outward and piercing the cheek-bone in front of the eye, whence, curving like a boar's tusk, it had slowly closed the jaws and locked them, rigid, set, as fixed as jaws of stone.

At first the animal had been able to gnaw; but as the tooth curved through the bones of the face and gradually tightened the jaws, the creature got less and less to eat, until, one day, creeping out of the burrow for food, the poor thing was unable to get back.

We seldom come upon the like of this. It is commoner than we think; but, as I have said, it is usually hidden away and quickly over. How often do we see a wild thing sick—a bird or other animal suffering from an accident, or dying, like this muskrat, because of some physical defect? The struggle between animals—the falling of the weak as prey to the strong—is ever before us; but this single-handed fight between the creature and Nature is a far rarer, silenter tragedy. Nature is too swift to allow us time for sympathy.

At best there is only a fighting chance in the meadow. Only strength and craft may win; only those who have all of their teeth. The muskrat with a single missing tooth never enters the real race of life at all. He slinks from some abandoned burrow, and, if the owl and mink are not watching, he dies alone in the grass, and we rarely know.

—Winter

To know much of the wild animals at home one must live near their haunts, with eyes and ears open, forever on the watch.
—A *Watcher in the Woods*

To Know Wild Animals

Soon there was a wake in one of the silvery roads, then a parting of waves, and stemming silently and evenly toward us, we saw the round, black head of a muskrat. ... A plank had drifted against the bank, and upon this the little creature scrambled out, as dry as a cat at home under the roaring kitchen stove. Down another road came a second muskrat, and, swimming across the open water at the dam, joined the firstcomer on the plank. They rubbed noses softly—the sweetest of all wild-animal greetings—and a moment afterward began to play together. They were out for a frolic, and the night was splendid. Keeping one eye open for owls, they threw off all caution, and swam and dived and chased each other through the water, with all the fun of boys in swimming.
—A *Watcher in the Woods*

Muskrats at Play

Finding wild bees, I think, would be good training for one intending to hunt hummingbirds' nests in the woods. ... Hummingbirds' nests are the gifts of the gods—rewards for patience and for gratitude because of commoner grants. My nests have invariably come ... by accident.
—A *Watcher in the Woods*

Finding Hummingbirds' Nests

Quail Hardships

Probably the life of no other of our winter birds is so full of hardship as is that of the quail, bob white. ... I have often heard the scattered, frightened families called together after a day of hard shooting; and once, in the old pasture to the north of Cubby Hollow, I saw the bevy assemble. ... It was long after sunset, but the snow so diffused the light that I could see pretty well. In climbing the fence into the pasture, I had started a rabbit, and was creeping up behind a low cedar, when a quail, very near me, whistled softly, *Whirl-ee!* The cedar was between us. *Whirl-ee, whirl-ee-gig!* she whistled again.

It was the sweetest bird-note I ever heard, being so low, so liquid, so mellow that I almost doubted if bob white could make it. But there she stood in the snow with head high, listening anxiously. Again she whistled, louder this time; and from the woods below came a faint answering call: *White!* The answer seemed to break a spell; and on three sides of me sounded other calls. At this the little signaler repeated her efforts, and each time the answer came louder and nearer. Presently something dark hurried by me over the snow and joined the quail I was watching. It was one of the covey that I had heard call from the woods.

Again and again the signal was sent forth until a third, fourth, and finally a fifth were grouped about the leader. There was just an audible twitter of welcome and gratitude exchanged as each new-comer made his appearance. Once more the whistle sounded; but this time there was no response across the silent field.

The quails made their way to a thick cedar that spread out over the ground, and, huddling together in a close bunch ... they murmured something soft and low among themselves. ... I crept away, sorry that even one had been taken from the little brood.

—*A Watcher in the Woods*

One of the most pathetic of all the wordless cries of the out-of-doors is the covey-call of the female quail at night, trying to gather together the scattered flock after the dogs are called off and the hunters have gone home.

—*A Watcher in the Woods*

The Pathetic Cry

From the barn to the orchard is no great journey; but it is the distance between two bird-lands. One must cross the Mississippi basin, the Rocky Mountains, or the Pacific Ocean to find a greater change in bird life than he finds in leaping the bars between the yard and the orchard.

—*A Watcher in the Woods*

Two Bird-Lands

If it is the bluebirds that bring the spring, the barn-swallows fetch the summer.

—*A Watcher in the Woods*

*The Swallows
Bring Summer*

The bluebirds ... are so gentle and refined in their voice and manner as to shed an atmosphere of good breeding about the whole yard. ... They are the first to return in the spring; the spring, rather, comes back with them. They are its wings.

—*A Watcher in the Woods*

Bluebirds and Spring

Birds and Dead Trees

If one wants to know what birds are about, especially the larger, more cautious species, let him get under cover near a tall dead oak or walnut, standing alone in the middle of open fields. Such a tree is the natural rest and lookout for every passer. Here comes the hawks to wait and watch; here the sentinel crows are posted while the flock pilfers corns and plugs melons; here the flicker and woodpeckers light for a quick lunch of grubs, ... here the flocking blackbirds swoop and settle, making the old tree look as if it had suddenly leaved out in mourning— ... and here the turkey-buzzards halt heavily in their gruesomely glorious flight. ... Not in a day's tramp will one see so many birds, and have such chances to observe them. ...

—*A Watcher in the Woods*

Swifts

Swifts are not as attractive as song-sparrows. They are sooty—worse than sooty sometimes; their clothes are too tight for them; and they are less musical than a small boy with "clappers." Nevertheless I could ill spare them from my family. They were the first birds I knew, my earliest home being so generous in its chimneys as to afford lodgings to several pairs of them. This summer they again share my fireside, squeaking, scratching, and thundering in the flue as they used to when, real goblins, they came scrambling down to peek and spy at me. I should miss them from the chimney as I should the song-sparrows from the meadow. They are above the grate, to be sure, while I am in front of it; but we live in the same house, and there is only a wall between us.

—*A Watcher in the Woods*

We have no Gilbert White. We have not had time to produce one. The union of man and nature which yields the naturalist of Selbourne is a process of time. Our soil and our sympathy are centuries savager than England's. We still look at our lands with the spirit of the ax; we are yet largely concerned with the contents of the gizzards of our birds. Shall the crows and cherry-birds be exterminated? the sparrows transported? the owls and hawks put behind bars? Not until the collectors at Washington pronounce upon these first questions can we hope for a naturalist who will find White's wonders in the chimney swallow.

—*A Watcher in the Woods*

Our Material Point of View

To know the pixy when one sees it, to call the long Latin name of the ragweed, to exclaim over the bobolink's song, to go into ecstasies at a glorious sunset, is not, necessarily to love nature at all. One who does all this sincerely, but who stuffs his ears to the din of the spring frogs, is in love with nature's pretty clothes, her dainty airs and fine ways. Her warm true heart lies deeper down.

—*A Watcher in the Woods*

To Truly Appreciate Nature

Take it the year round, the deadest trees in the woods are the livest and fullest of fruit—for the naturalist. ... Sooner or later, every dead tree in the neighborhood finds a place in my note-book. They are all named and mentioned, some over and over—my list of Immortals, ...

—*A Watcher in the Woods*

Hollow Trees

Toad Philosophy

Just after sunset, when the fireflies light up and the crickets and katydids begin to chirp, the toad that sleeps under my front step hops out of bed, kicks the sand off his back, and takes a long look at the weather. He seems to think as he sits here on the gravel walk, so sober and still, with his face turned skyward. What does he think about? Is he listening to the chorus of the crickets, to the whipporwills, or is it for supper he is planning? ... Who knows? Someday perhaps we shall have a batrachian psychology and I shall understand what it is that my door-step lodger turns over in his mind as he watches the coming of the stars.

—*A Watcher in the Woods*

Nature's Smile

A bent, rheumatic, hoary old orchard is nature's smile in the agony of her civilization.

—*A Watcher in the Woods*

Swamp-Gums

The deliberate purpose of a swamp-gum, through its hundred years of life, is to grow as big as possible, that it may hollow out accordingly. They are the natural home-makers of the swamps that border the rivers and creeks in southern New Jersey. What would the coons, the turkey-buzzards, and the owls do without them? The wild bees believe the gums are especially built for them. No white-painted hive, with its disappearing squares, offers half as much safety to these freebooters of the summer seas as the gums, open-hearted, thick-walled and impregnable.

—*A Watcher in the Woods*

The Skunk

The skunk wants a champion. Some one ought to spend an entire October moon with him and give us the better side of his character. If some one would take the trouble to get well acquainted with him at home, it might transpire that we have grievously abused and avoided him.

—*A Watcher in the Woods*

An Animal's Strong Points

An animal's strong points usually supplement each other; its well-developed powers are in line with its needs and mode of life. So, by the very demands of his peculiar life, the beaver has become chief among all the animal engineers, his specialty being dams. He can make a good slide for logging, but of the construction of speedways he knows absolutely nothing. The rabbit, on the other hand, is a runner. He can swim if he is obliged to. His interests, however, lie mostly in his heels, and hence in his highways. So Bunny has become an expert roadmaker. He cannot build a house, nor dig even a respectable den; he is unable to climb, and his face is too flat for hole-gnawing; but turn him loose in a brambly, briery wilderness, and he will soon thread the trackless wastes with a network of roads, and lay it open to his nimble feet as the sky lies open to the swallow's wings.

—*A Watcher in the Woods*

The White-footed Mouse

Hesperomys is the rather woodsy name of the white-footed or deer-mouse, a shy, timid little creature dwelling in every wood, who, notwith- standing his abundance, is an utter stranger to most of us. We are more familiar with his tracks ... than with even those of the squirrel and rabbit. His is that tiny double trail galloped across the snowy paths in the woods. We see them sprinkled over the snow every-where; but when have we seen the feet that left them? Here goes a line of the wee prints from a hole in the snow near a stump over to the butt of a large pine. Whitefoot has gone for proven-der to one of his storehouses among the roots of the pine; or maybe a neighbor lives here, and he has left his nest of bird-feathers in the stump to make a friendly call after the storm.

—*A Watcher in the Woods*

Squirrels and Weather

The woodsmen and other wiseacres say that the squirrels never build the tree-top nests except in anticipation of a mild winter. But weather wisdom, when the gray squirrel is the source, is as little wise as that which comes from Washington or the almanac. I have found the nests in the tree-tops in the coldest, fiercest winters.

—*A Watcher in the Woods*

Hyla with Spring in His Heart

The bluebird comes because he has seen the spring; Hyla comes because he has the spring in his heart.

—*A Watcher in the Woods*

The Jumping Mouse

Zapus, the jumping mouse, the exquisite little fellow with the long tail and kangaroo legs, has made his nest of leaves and grass down in the ground, where he lies in a tiny ball just out of the frost's reach, fast asleep. He will be plowed out of bed next spring, if his nest is in a field destined for corn or melons; for *Zapus* is sure to oversleep. The bluebirds, robins, and song-sparrows will have been back for weeks, the fields will be turning green, and as for the flowers, there will be a long procession of them started, before this pretty sleepy-head rubs his eyes, uncurls himself, and digs his way out to see the new spring morning.

—*A Watcher in the Woods*

The Night Eye

Nights of watching, when every fallen leaf is a sentinel and every moonbeam a spy, will let us into some secrets about the ponds and fields that the sun, old and all-seeing as he is, will never know. Our eyes were made for daylight; but I think if the anatomists tried they might find the rudiments of a third, a night eye, behind the other two.

—*A Watcher in the Woods*

Meadowlark in Winter

Nothing seems so utterly homeless and solitary as a meadowlark after the winter nightfall. In the middle of a wide, snow-covered pasture one will occasionally spring from under your feet, scattering the snow that covered him, and go whirring away through the dusk, lost instantly in the darkness—a single little life in the wild, bleak wilderness of winter fields!

—*A Watcher in the Woods*

The Protectively Colored Frogs

The entire frog family is protectively colored. ... They all carry fern-seed in their pockets and go invisible. Notice the wood-frog with his tan suit and black cheeks. He is a mere sound as he hops about over the brown leaves. I have had him jump out of the way of my feet and vanish while I stared hard at him. He lands with legs extended, purposely simulating the shape of the ragged, broken leaves, and offers, as the only clue for one's baffled eyes, the moist glisten as his body dissolves against the dead brown of the leaf-carpet. The tree-toad, *Hyla versicolor*, still more strikingly blends with his surroundings, for, ... he can change color to match the bark upon which he sits. More than once, in climbing apple trees, I have put my hand upon a tree-toad, not distinguishing it from the patches of gray-green lichen upon the limbs.

—*A Watcher in the Woods*

Birds and Man

If we should let the birds have their way, they would voluntarily fall into civilized, if not domesticated habits. They have no deep-seated hostility toward us; ... The way they forgive and forget, ... ought to shame us. They sing over every acre that we reclaim, as if we had saved it for them ... they girdle the apple-trees for grubs, and gallop over the whole wide sky for gnats and flies—squaring their account, if may be, for cherries, orchards, and chimneys.

—*A Watcher in the Woods*

Very green babies of all kinds are queer, uncertain, indescribable creations—faith generators. But the greenest, homeliest, unlikeliest, babiest babies I ever encountered were these two in the hole. I wish Walt Whitman had seen them. He would have written a poem.

—*A Watcher in the Woods*

Young Barred Owls

Not in a day's tramp will one see so many birds, and have such chances to observe them, as in a single hour, when the sun is rising or setting, in the neighborhood of some great, gaunt tree that has died of years of lonesomeness, or been smitten by a bolt from the summer clouds.

—*A Watcher in the Woods*

Where to See Birds

In fact, I never saw a redstart who seemed to know that we humans ought to be dreaded. These birds are as innocent of suspicion as when they came up to Adam to be named.

—*A Watcher in the Woods*

The Innocence of Redstarts

American naturalist and specialist in tropical
American ornithology; winner of the John
Burroughs Medal for *Nature Through Tropical
Windows* (1983)

A Naturalist's Philosophy of Nature

Through intimate association with the
living things around us, we reach out beyond
the narrow human sphere into the larger natural
world that surrounds and sustains us. We
develop toward this world an attitude, often
intensely personal, that with time and thought
may grow into a world view or philosophy of
nature; possibly, if held with fervor and capable
of strongly influencing our conduct, it might be
called a religion. Perhaps to have developed
such a comprehensive outlook, especially if it be
hopeful and sustaining rather than gloomy or
despairing, is the most important outcome of
long association with nature.

—*Nature Through Tropical Windows*

The Attractiveness of Small Animals

Others may go to Africa to see elephants,
giraffes, lions, and ostriches, or to Yellowstone
Park to meet grizzly bears and bison; to me, the
much smaller creatures that surround me are more
attractive and interesting. Their activities tend to
be more varied; they are more creative; and they
can be watched at close range with less danger. A
comparison of great and small animals gives the
advantage to the latter on almost every point
except size and power.

—*Nature Through Tropical Windows*

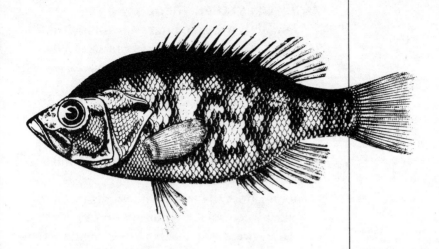

If the biblical account of Paradise is accurate, it was where guileless newly created man dwelt in perfect health and safety with nothing between his naked skin and his environment. This suggests an ecological definition of paradise as a habitat where we might thrive in such perfect harmony with our surroundings, living and lifeless, that no insulation of any kind would be needed. Although in our present troubled world you might search in vain for a place that is wholly paradisiacal, a tropical valley just high enough to take the edge off tropical heat, out of the path of hurricanes and shielded by a mountain rampart from persistent winds, covered with flourishing vegetation and not too densely populated by man, is as close to paradise as most of us can aspire to. ... And if through his open windows the dweller in such a valley can watch flowering trees, lovely birds, and other creatures, what more can he reasonably desire?

—*Nature Through Tropical Windows*

Where Paradise Is

STANWELL-FLETCHER, THEODORA C. (1906–)
Naturalist, writer and traveler with husband,
John F. Stanwell-Fletcher in British Columbia,
Canada; collector of animals for science mu-
seum related in book, *Driftwood Valley*, the
winner of the John Burroughs Medal (1948)

Song of the Dipper

November 14
 The last daylight faded and the world was
locked in the silence and glittering snow and
moonlight of the early northern night. Then,
suddenly, outside ... a burst of rippling notes ...
a clear, sweet song ... on a bitter night with the
temperature at zero and two feet of snow. It
couldn't be possible. But the music was still
there, now just above the cabin roof, now down
over the lake. We rushed out and there by the
open water patch below ... three ... gray
dippers, or water ouzels, with short bobbing
tails. Neither of us had an idea that any bird
ever sang at night in the depths of winter, much
less a northern one. In vivid moonlight we
could see them ... dipping and bobbing on rocks
in the cold shining water—and singing. Their
song echoed back and forth so that all the lake
was ringing with it. When we went inside again
the birds flew above our roof and poured their
music down on us. No European nightingale,
singing in a hot lush summer evening ever wove
the spell of enchantment that the dippers did
with those crystal tinkles, which matched so
perfectly the icy purity of the winter night.
         —*Driftwood Valley*

January 6

As usual we traveled in complete restful
silence. To be able to gain thoughts and impressions all one's own, unsullied by vocal observations from companions, exactly as if one were
walking by oneself, is sheer pleasure. This gift of
quiet is one which inhabitants of the civilized
world don't possess. They don't understand that
impressions are far more impressive if no word is
spoken. Besides, when one travels a wilderness,
being quiet so that one can really use one's
senses of sight and hearing and feeling is a
necessary safeguard. ...

—*Driftwood Valley*

Wolf Song

February 15

Utter silence, a deathlike hush over the land, and then, from somewhere below, came a sound that made our hearts stand still. Like a breath of wind, rising slowly, softly, clearly to a high, lovely note of sadness and longing; dying down on two distinct notes so low that our human ears could scarcely catch them. It rose and died, again and again. A wolf singing the beauty of the night, singing it as no human voice had ever done, calling on a mate to share the beauty of it. ... Over and over it sang, so tenderly and exquisitely that it seemed as if the voice were calling to me and I could hardly keep from crying. The whole wilderness was musical with it. After an interval ... from far away across the eastern hills came a soft, distinct, answering call. Three times more the wolf below us sang and was answered. Gradually the other voice grew nearer and nearer, until we thought that the two must have come together, for the sudden quiet was not broken again.

Then I knew that I was shivering and my arm, which J. had been grasping, was almost paralyzed.

J. was ... saying: "Gad, what luck! What marvelous luck! I've heard wolves howling in India and the Arctic, but I never heard the like of that!"

—*Driftwood Valley*

August 16

Autumn. Every day now across the still green
waters ... we hear the voice of the Pacific loon—
that ghostly, haunting, wailing "oh-h-h, oh-h-h-h,
ooh-ooh." Like a woman crying hopelessly,
endlessly. Like a baby bear who has lost its mother.
Like the faint far-off foghorn of a ship at sea. Like
the mournful sigh of wind in a pine tree. We have
a pair staying with us for a time... When they're
separated they begin calling and answering in
those voices which haunt one day and night, and
of which, one can never hear enough. ...
                                    —*Driftwood Valley*

STEINHART, PETER (1943–   )
Columnist with *Audubon* magazine and lecturer at
Stanford University; author of *Tracks in the Sky*

To spend childhood days along creek banks is
to be drawn into the wider world. A creek reaches
upward into the hills and mountains, where clouds
brood and gods bluster. It reaches down to the low-
lands and the fat old rivers, sad and murky with
the silt of experience. A creek teaches one the
curve of the Earth, the youthful swell of mountains, the age of the seas. Above all, a creek offers
the mind a chance to penetrate the alien world of
water and think like a tadpole or a trout. That is
one of the great experiences of otherness, one of
the leaps of perception that makes us human and
allows us to live with dream and obscurity. What
drifts in creek water is the possibility of other worlds
inside and above our own. Poet Robert Frost
wrote, "It flows between us, over us, and with us.
And it is time, strength, tone, light, life and love."
                        —*From an essay, The Meaning of Creeks*

*The Haunting Voice
of the Loon*

*The World of
Creek Waters*

STEPHENS, JAMES (1882–1950)
  Irish poet and fiction writer

Little Things

  Little things, that run and quail,
  And die, in silence and despair!
  Little things, that fight and fail,
  And fall, on sea, and earth, and air!
  All trapped and frightened little things,
  The mouse, the coney, hear our prayer!
  As we forgive those done to us,
  —The lamb, the linnet, and the hare—
  Forgive us all our trespasses,
  Little creatures everywhere!
                    —*James Stephens Collected Poems*

STRINGER, ARTHUR (1874–1950)
  American poet

The Real Captive

  Mourn not him who hates his cage too well
  And beats against the bars row by row,
  But weep for him who learns to love his cell
  And when the door swings wide, is loath to go.
                    —New York Times, *October 29, 1947*

SUTRAS
  Ancient Hindu aphoristic manuals, possibly
  written 500 to 200 B.C.

True Brotherhood

  A man should wander about treating all
  creatures as he himself would be treated.
                    —*Sutra-Kritanga Sutra 1:11:33*

SUTTON, GEORGE M. (1898–1982)

American ornithologist, bird artist, explorer, educator, curator of ornithology and author; winner of the John Burroughs Medal for *Iceland Summer* (1962)

The beginnings of an ornithologist's life are interesting in that they preface, and to some extent, account for the journeyings and escapades of later years.

—*Birds in the Wilderness*

The Boyhood of the Birdman

A Screech Owl may chuckle, coo like a dove, or grunt like a tiny, arboreal pig; but his familiar song is a smoothly quavering whistle, so gently begun that it is well-nigh finished before we realize that our spine has tingled, our eyebrows lifted, and head turned, in response to the insistant cry.

—*Birds in the Wilderness*

The Silver-voiced Screech Owl

TAYLOR, WALTER P. (dates unknown)
American biologist, mammalogist, author and educator

Biology—
Stepchild of the Sciences

Anybody who has got so far as the sophomore year knows that science is all-inclusive, a sort of continuum, being man's total efforts to learn something definite about the universe he is living in. As one grows in insight, he learns that there are no rigid boundaries between the abstracted aspects of reality we know as physics, chemistry, geology, botany, zoology, etc. Each fades into the other. Unfortunately, this is not always the current conception. One has only to read the daily papers to awaken, with something of a start, to find that, for many persons, some in very high places, present day science includes, for practical purposes, only physics, chemistry, engineering, and mathematics. If biology rates at all, it is in the apocrypha at the back of the book.

—*Is Biology Obsolete?*

TEAL, JOHN AND MILDRED (1929–)
American writers and scientists

The Hostile Environment
of the Sargasso

From a human viewpoint, few more hostile environments exist than the little-known, dark, desert waters of the bathypelagic Sargasso. Even the moon is barely less hospitable. Both share conditions that necessitate continuous life-support systems for humans. The moon offers a solid substrate, earth—and sunrises, and a vista extending to millions of light years. All these amenities are lacking in the dark waters far under the Sargasso's slowly circulating surface.

—*The Sargasso Sea*

Many evolutionary inventions are specific for food getting. Many others show two faces. Speed can as well be used to escape becoming food as it does to gain it. Lights can be used to blind predator as well as lure prey. How not to be eaten is no less important than how to eat. With a sea full of strange creatures with ravenous appetites and highly complex mechanisms for satisfying these appetites, time has provided counter-balancing mechanisms. If it did not, life would vanish from the Sargasso.

—*The Sargasso Sea*

TEALE, EDWIN WAY (1899–1980)
American writer, naturalist, photographer, amateur entomologist and scholar; winner of the John Burroughs Medal for *Near Horizons* (1943)

Like the toad that lives under the corncrib, the birds that perch in the ancient apple trees, and the bat that flies like a windblown leaf over the swamp at twilight, the mole is part of the web of … life. Beetle grubs form an important item on its diet. Beneath the soil, this tunnelmaker plays its role in maintaining the balance of nature just as toad and bird and bat do on the ground and in the air.

—*Near Horizons*

It is through moods, rather than through facts or dates or names, that the most vivid memories of the past return.

—*Near Horizons*

What We Miss in Life

At one time or another there comes to most of us a realization of how much will remain undone when the world ends for us. Even if we circle the globe, how many sights and sounds and smells we still shall miss! Even if we become acquainted with millions, how many possible friends we shall never know! Even if we devour whole libraries, how many volumes will remain unread! No matter how full, our lives inevitably must remain, in some respects, random and incomplete.

—*Near Horizons*

Night, Loneliness and Passing Time

Nightime is never frivolous. It may appear majestic or brooding, or friendly or filled with terror. But it is never trivial. The swift disappearance of diurnal landmarks; the enveloping hush of this transitional hour; the commencement of the slow, night-long glide of the stars above my garden tree, all these ... emphasize the essential loneliness of the individual and the relentless flowing of time.

—*Near Horizons*

The Music of Night Insects

The music of the night insects has been familiar to every generation of men since the earliest humans; it has come down like a Greek chorus chanting around the actors throughout the course of human history.

—*Near Horizons*

Man has a choice of action; the insects are almost exclusively guided by instinct. Thus they, far better than man, reflect the real character and outlook of Nature. In spite of all the inhumanity of man to man, the sum total of kindly impulses is greater among humans than among any of these creatures. ... The ferocity of the natural world ... is ... in the warfare which swirls endlessly across the battlefield of my rosebush.

—*Near Horizons*

The Ferocity of the Natural World

What Iliads and Odysseys the adventures of the insects would present, if these small creatures wrote books! What panoramas of change the chronicle of their millions of years on earth would reveal! History, written from the standpoint of the insects would record the rise and disappearance of whole faunas and floras. It would picture the shift of seas and the formation of mountain ranges. It would tell, from the very beginning, the story of the Mississippi and the Amazon. It would record the earliest days of man.

—*Near Horizons*

The Unwritten History of the Insects

If a man beats his wife, squanders his fortune, or jumps off a bridge ... the world will understand, if it doesn't condone. But if he begins to spend his leisure time ... with the insects, ... people may condone but they rarely understand.

—*Near Horizons*

People and the Study of Insects

The Chrysalis of the
Monarch Butterfly

Few things produced by insects are more beautiful than the chrysalis of the Monarch. As I saw it that morning on the maple twig, it was jade green and decorated with a black line and dots of purest shining gold. Within this husk of chitin, the pupa lived and breathed, a half-creature neither larva nor butterfly but something between.

—Near Horizons

Hatred for
Harmless Creatures

Imagining the worst about wild creatures around us, is a tendency of mankind. American pioneers believed the harmless caterpillars of the Mourning Cloak butterfly were ... poisonous. The harmless hieroglyphics of the leftminers, those tiny grubs which make their curved and looping trails in plant tissues, were once considered the signatures of evil spirits. Bats were long accused of eating hams; dragonflies were thought to sew up little boys' ears; toads have been blamed for warts. The false propaganda of the centuries has stimulated hatred for harmless forms of life.

—Near Horizons

Sounds That Link
Us to Wild Animals

Sounds link us to dumb creatures even more than the observations of our eyes. The bird crying above her disturbed nest, or the animal whimpering in pain, affects us far more than does the fish which silently gasps in a death-struggle out of water.

—Near Horizons

TENNYSON, ALFRED LORD (1809–1892)
English poet

Flower in the crannied wall,
I pluck you out of the crannies,
I hold you here, root and all, in my hand,
Little flower—but if I could understand
What you are, root and all, and all in all
I should know what God and man is.
—The Pocket Book of Verse

Flower in the Crannied Wall

He clasps the crag with crooked hands;
Close to the sun in lonely lands,
Ring'd with the azure world, he stands.

The wrinkled sea beneath him crawls;
He watches from his mountain walls,
And like a thunderbolt he falls.
—Poems of Tennyson

The Eagle

TERRES, JOHN K. (1905–   )
American writer, naturalist and journal-keeper;
former editor, *Audubon* magazine and author of
*The Audubon Society Encyclopedia of North
American Birds*; winner of the John Burroughs
Medal for *From Laurel Hill To Siler's Bog: The
Walking Adventures of a Naturalist* (1971)

In nature, the cost of being rare, beautiful,
or extra large, often comes high. Men prize the
rare, the beautiful, and the unusual, and they
kill to possess the prize.
—Unpublished Journals of a Naturalist

The High Cost of Being Unusual

Requirements of the Naturalist

What is a naturalist? What is he like? What are his interests, his philosophies? his pursuits? His journals may not always tell, but there are requirements if he is to be a gatherer of those original observations that build his knowledge. The most important equipment he carries is his silence, his ability to walk with stealth, for the Japanese proverb says, "Walk softly and go far."

A naturalist must have patience, born of his curiosity, to stand or to sit for hours if necessary in any weather. This he will endure to learn some fact new to him or to add to knowledge he already has, say of a bluebird, a fox, a snake, or a butterfly. He must use to his utmost his eyes, his ears, his sense of touch, and his sense of smell. He must have the power of complete concentration and awareness of everything going on around him. In this way, the natural world is revealed to him, or, as much of it as he is capable of absorbing.

I have learned that when on a walk—out to observe, not to teach—that I must be alone or with one companion at most. And that companion must be sympathetic to the world around us. He must be a partner in silence much of the time, except for note-taking and occasional conferences over something either of us may have seen that needs to be interpreted or needs further information, or confirmation.

My equipment for observing is simple—a pair of binoculars and a notebook and pen to set down observations swiftly and concisely—to sketch a wild bird, a frog, a toad, an insect, a tree, a leaf, a wildflower. I dress for the weather, in durable brown clothing and shoes—canvas shoes in summer that dry quickly after wading a

river, a creek, a pond, and a utility bag slung
from my shoulders with a compass for untracked
woods, a knife, a coil of wire or of string,
matches, and a bar of chocolate for emergencies.
And so equipped I take to the obscure trails of a
naturalist's "roads to adventure."

—*An Introduction to Unpublished
Journals of a Naturalist*

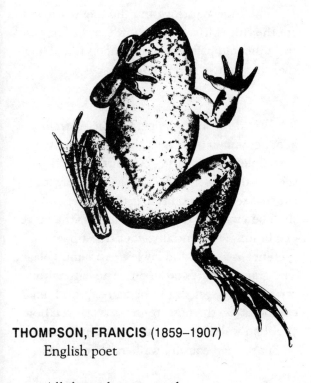

THOMPSON, FRANCIS (1859–1907)
English poet

All things by immortal power
Near or far
Hiddenly
To each other linked are,
That thou canst not stir a flower
Without troubling a star.

—*The Mistress of Vision*

Oneness of the Universe

197

THOREAU, HENRY DAVID (1817–1862)
American essayist, poet, naturalist and philosopher

Better the Living Than the Dead

Every creature is better alive than dead, men and moose and pine trees, and he who understands it aright will rather preserve its life than destroy it.

—*Chesuncook*

The True Spirits of the Snowstorm

The snow buntings and the tree sparrows are the true spirits of the snow-storm. They are the animated beings that ride upon it and have their life in it.

—*Winter*

Grammar and Expression

When I hear the hypercritical quarreling about grammar and style, the position of the participles ... stretching or contracting every speaker to certain rules ... I see they forget that the first requisite and rule is that expression shall be vital and natural, as much as the voice of a brute. ... Essentially, your truest poetic sentence is as free and lawless as a lamb's bleat. The grammarian is often one who can neither cry nor laugh, yet thinks he can express human emotions. So the posture-masters tell you how you shall walk, turning your toes out excessively ... but so the beautiful walkers are not made.

—*Winter*

The Worst Kind of a Tick

The worst kind of a tick to get under your skin is yourself in an irritable mood.

—*Winter*

I love Nature partly because she is not a man, but a retreat from him. None of his institutions control or pervade her. Here a different kind of right prevails. In her midst I can be glad with an entire gladness. If this world were all man, I could not stretch myself, I should lose all hope. He is restraint; she is freedom to me. He makes me wish for another world; she makes me content with this. None of the joys she supplies is subject to his rules and definitions. What he touches he taints. In thought he moralizes. ... How infinite and pure the least pleasure of which nature is basis compared with the congratulations of mankind! The joy which nature yields is like that afforded by frank words of one we love.

—*Winter*

Nature—
A Retreat from Man

A man must attend to nature closely for many years to know when as well as where, to look for his objects, since he must always anticipate her a little. Young men have not learned the phases of nature. They do not know what constitutes a year, or that one year is like another. I would know when in the year to expect certain thoughts and moods, as the sportsman knows when to look for plover.

—*Autumn*

Learn to
Anticipate Nature

September 26, 1840 ... The increasing scarlet and yellow tints around the meadows and river remind me of the opening of a vast flower bud. They are the petals of its corolla, which are of the width of the valley. It is the flower of autumn, whose expanding bud just begins to blush.

—*Autumn*

The Flowers of Autumn

Why Birds Are Creatures of Omen

Birds were very naturally made the subject of augury, for they are but borderers upon the earth, creatures of another and more ethereal element than our existence can be supported in, which seem to flit between us and the unexplored.

—*Autumn*

Where Your Happiness Lies

A man dwells in his native valley like a corolla in its calyx, like an acorn in its cup. Here, of course, is all that you love, all that you expect, all that you are. Here is your bride-elect, as close to you as she can be got. Here is all the best and the worst you can imagine. What more do you want? Foolish people think that what they imagine is somewhere else. That stuff is not made in any factory but their own.

—*Autumn*

The Necessary Path

Each man's necessary path, though as obscure and apparently uneventful as that of a beetle in the grass, is the way to the deepest joys he is susceptible of. Though he converses only with moles and fungi, and disgraces his relatives, it is not matter, if he knows what is steel to his flint.

—*Autumn*

Swamp Knowledge

... You must be conversant with things for a long time to know much about them, like the moss which has hung from the spruce, and as the partridge and the rabbit are acquainted with the thickets, and at length have acquired the color of the places they frequent. If the man of science can put all his knowledge into propositions, the woodman has a great deal of incommunicable knowledge. ...

—*Autumn*

The True Value of What We See

I think the man of science makes the mistake, and the mass of mankind along with him, to suppose that you should give your chief attention to the phenomenon which excites you, as something independent of you, and not as it is related to you. The important fact is its effect on me. The man of science thinks I have no business to see anything else but just what he defines the rainbow to be, but I care not whether my vision is a wakening thought or dream remembered, whether it is seen in the light or in the dark. It is the subject of the vision, the truth alone that concerns me. The philosopher for whom rainbows ... can be explained away never saw them.

—*Autumn*

Sound Growth

I am struck by the fact that the more slowly trees grow at first, the sounder they are at the core, and I think the same is true of human beings. We do not wish to see children precocious, making great strides in their early years, like sprouts producing a soft and perishable timber, but better if they expand slowly at first, as if contending with difficulties, and so are solidified and perfected. Such trees continue and expand with nearly equal rapidity to an extreme old age.

—*Autumn*

Labor That Serves the Writer

Hard and steady, and engrossing labor with the hands, especially out of doors, is invaluable to the literary man and serves him directly. Here I have been for six days surveying in the woods, and yet when I get home at evening somewhat weary at last, and beginning to feel that I have nerves, I find myself more susceptible than usual to the finest influences, as music and poetry. The very air can intoxicate me, or the least sight or sound, as if my finer senses had acquired an appetite by their fast.

—*Autumn*

Beech Leaves and Beech Bark

November 2, 1853—The beech leaves have all fallen except some about the lower part of the trees, and they make a fine thick bed on the ground. They are very beautiful, fine and perfect leaves, unspotted, not eaten by insects, of a handsome, clear leather color, like a book bound in calf, crisp and elastic. They cover the ground so perfectly and cleanly as to tempt you to recline on it, and admire the beauty of the smooth boles ... covered with lichens of various colors. ... They impress you as full of health and vigor, so that their bark can hardly contain their spirits, but lies in folds or wrinkles about their ankles like a sack, with the ... wrinkles of fat, or infancy.

—*Autumn*

The Fearless Sparrow

I once had a sparrow alight upon my shoulder ... and I felt that I was more distinguished ... than ... by any epaulet I could have worn.

—*Walden*

We can only live healthfully the life the gods assign us. I must receive my life as passively as the willow leaf that flutters over the brook. I must not be for myself but God's work, and that is always good. I will wait the breezes patiently, and grow as they shall determine. My fate cannot but be grand so. We may live the life of a plant or an animal without living an animal life. This constant and universal content of the animal comes of resting quietly in God's palm. I feel as if I could at any time resign my life and the responsibility into God's hands and become as innocent and free from care as a plant or stone.

—*Early Spring in Massachusetts*

Resting Quietly in God's Palm

March 13, 1819. I cannot easily forget the beauty of those terrestrial browns in the rain yesterday. The withered grass was not of that very, pale, hoary brown that it is today now that it is dry and lifeless; but being perfectly saturated and dripping with the rain, the whole hillside seemed to reflect a certain yellowish light so that you looked around for the sun in the midst of the storm.

—*Early Spring in Massachusetts*

Brown Grass in the Rain

I rejoice that there are owls. Let them do the idiotic and maniacal hooting for men. It is a sound admirably suited to swamps and twilight woods which no day illustrates, suggesting a vast and undeveloped nature which men have not recognized. ...

—*Walden*

The Hooting of Owls

**Destruction
of Woodlands**

How can you expect the birds to sing when their groves are cut down?

—*Walden*

**King of the
Pumpkin Patch**

... I would rather sit on a pumpkin and have it all to myself, then be crowded on a velvet cushion.

—*Walden*

**The Flavor
of Huckleberries**

If you would know the flavor of huckleberries, ask the cowboy or the partridge.

—*Walden*

Whip-poor-wills

Regularly at half past seven ... after the evening train had gone by, the whip-poor-wills chanted their vespers for half an hour, sitting on a stump by my door, or upon the ridgepole of the house. ... Sometimes I heard four or five at once in different parts of the wood, by accident one a bar behind another, and so near me that I distinguished not only the cluck after each note, but often that singular buzzing sound like a fly in a spider's web, only proportionately louder.

—*Walden*

**The Standards of
Birds and Flowers**

... if the birds and flowers had tried me by their standard, I should not have been found wanting.

—*Walden*

**The Motions
of a Squirrel**

... all the motions of a squirrel, even in the most solitary recesses of the forest, imply spectators as much as those of a dancing girl. ...

—*Walden*

Still grows the vivacious lilac ... after the door and lintel and the sill are gone, unfolding its sweet-scented flowers each spring, to be plucked by the musing traveler; planted and tended once by children's hands, in front yard plots—not standing by wall-sides in retired pastures, and giving place to new-rising forests. ... Little did the dusky children think that which they stuck in the ground in the shadow of the house and daily watered, would root itself so, and outlive them ... and tell their story faintly to the lone wanderer a half century after they had grown up and died—blossoming as fair and smelling as sweet, as in that first spring.
—*Walden*

Lilacs and Lost Generations

I went to the woods because I wished to live deliberately, to front only the essential facts of life, and see if I could not learn what it had to teach, and not, when I came to die, discover that I had not lived.
—*Walden*

Simplicity in Life

... the man who goes alone can start today; but he who travels, with another must wait till that other is ready, and it may be a long time before they get off.
—*Walden*

Travel Alone

It would be well, perhaps, if we were to spend more of our days and nights without any obstructions between us and the celestial bodies. ... Birds do not sing in caves, nor do doves cherish their innocence in dovecots.
—*Walden*

On Living Out-of-Doors

What Determines One's Fate	What a man thinks of himself, that it is which determines, or rather indicates, his fate. —*Walden*
Travel—Local	I have traveled a good deal in Concord. ... —*Walden*
The True Harvest	... If the day and night are such that you greet them with joy, and life emits a fragrance like flowers and sweet-scented herbs, is more elastic, more starry, more immortal—that is your success. ... The true harvest of my daily life is somewhat as intangible and indescribable as the tints of morning or evening. It is a little stardust caught, a segment of the rainbow which I have clutched. ... —*Walden*
The Tonic of Wildness	We need the tonic of wildness—to wade sometimes in marshes where the bittern and meadow hen lurk, and hear the booming of the snipe; to smell the whispering sedge where only some wilder and more solitary fowl builds her nest, ... —*Walden*
Fulfillment	... if one advances confidently in the direction of his dreams, and endeavors to live the life he has imagined, he will meet with a success unexpected in common hours. ... If you have built castles in the air, ... put the foundations under them. —*Walden*

If a man does not keep pace with his companions, perhaps it is because he hears a different drummer.

—*Walden*

Setting Our Own Pace

You need only sit still long enough in some attractive spot in the woods that all its inhabitants may exhibit themselves to you by turns.

—*Walden*

To Observe Wildlife

What is a country without rabbits and partridges? They are ... of the very hue and substance of Nature, nearest allied to leaves and to the ground— ... It is hardly as if you had seen a wild creature when a rabbit or a partridge bursts away, only a natural one, as much to be expected as rustling leaves. ...

—*Walden*

Rabbits and Partridges

... Why is it that a bucket of water soon becomes putrid, but frozen remains sweet forever? It is commonly said that this is the difference between the affections and the intellect.

—*Walden*

Affections and Intellect

... The day is an epitome of the year. The night is the winter, the morning and evening are the spring and fall, and the noon is the summer.

—*Walden*

Day—
An Epitome of the Year

Live in the Present

We should be blessed if we lived in the present always, and took advantage of every accident that befell us, like the grass which confesses the influence of the slightest dew that falls on it; ...

—*Walden*

The Purity of Walden Pond

... Walden is a perfect forest mirror,... Nothing so fair, so pure ... as a lake perchance, lies on the surface of the earth. Sky water. It needs no fence. Nations come and go without defiling it. It is a mirror which no stone can crack, whose quicksilver will never wear off, whose gilding Nature continually repairs; no storms, no dust, can dim its surface ever fresh; ...

—*Walden*

Books, the Treasure Wealth of the World

Books are the treasured wealth of the world and the fit inheritance of generations and nations. ... They have no cause of their own to plead, but while they enlighten and sustain the reader his common sense will not refuse them.

—*Walden*

The Written Word

... A written word is the choicest of relics. It is ... more intimate with us and more universal than any other work of art. It is the work of art nearest to life itself. ...

—*Walden*

The Influence of Books

How many a man has dated a new era in his life from the reading of a book!

—*Walden*

To read well, that is, to read true books in a true spirit, is a noble exercise, and one that will task the reader more than any exercise which the customs of the day esteem.

—*Walden*

To Read Well

Most men ... are so occupied with the factitious cares and ... coarse labors of life that its finer fruits cannot be plucked by them.

—*Walden*

The Cost of Our Labors

... making yourselves sick, that you may lay up something against a sick day. ...

—*Walden*

Our Civilized Illness

The mass of men lead lives of quiet desperation.

—*Walden*

The Lives of Most Men

It is never too late to give up our prejudices.

—*Walden*

Prejudices

To be a philosopher is not merely to have subtle thoughts, nor even to found a school, but so to love wisdom as to live according to its dictates, a life of simplicity, independence, magnanimity and trust.

—*Walden*

To Be a Philosopher

... a taste for the beautiful is most cultivated out of doors, ...

—*Walden*

A Taste for the Beautiful

Life's Disappointments

I long ago lost a hound, a bay horse, and a turtle dove, and am still on their trail. Many are the travelers I have spoken concerning them, describing their tracks and what calls they answered to. I have met one or two who heard the hound, and the tramp of the horse, and even seen the dove disappear behind a cloud, and they seemed as anxious to recover them as if they had lost them themselves.

—*Walden*

Life and Death in Nature

Every part of nature teaches that the passing away of one life is the making room for another. ...

—*The Journals of Henry D. Thoreau*

TORREY, BRADFORD (1843–1912)
American naturalist, ornithologist and author

Neighborliness of Crows

... The cawing of a dozen or two of crows, who were talking politics among the pines on the New Hampshire hillside, affected me most agreeably. There was something of real neighborliness about it. I would gladly have taken a hand in the discussion, if they would have let me. ...

—*Nature's Invitation*

The Wisdom of Trees

There is no tree but knows a thing or two. Every kind has a wisdom of its own. *Experientia docet* is true of them as of us. ...

—*Nature's Invitation*

To all men of science, though they be nothing but amateurs and dabsters, rarity is one of the cardinal virtues of a specimen.

—*Nature's Invitation*

Rarity a Virtue

The ways of shrewd people are hard to understand; and in all New England there is no shrewder Yankee than the crow.

—*Birds in the Bush*

The Unfathomable Crow

Why should men ... pronounce anything worthless merely because *they* can do nothing about it? ... Here is a worthy neighbor of mine whom I hear every summer complaining of the chicory plants which disfigure the roadside in front of her windows. She wishes they were exterminated, every one of them. ... But I never pass this spot in August ... without seeing that hers is only one side of the story. My approach is sure to startle a few goldfinches ... to whom these scraggly herbs are quite as useful as my excellent lady's apple-trees and pear-trees are to her. I watch them as they circle about in musical undulations and then drop down again to finish their repast ... in spite of its unsightliness, the chicory is not a weed—its use has been discovered.

—*Birds in the Bush*

The Value of Weeds

The Insanity of Bird-Watching

Take a gun on your shoulder and go wandering about the woods all day ... and you will be looked upon with respect ... or stand by the hour at the end of a fishing pole, catching nothing but mosquito-bites, and your neighbors will think no ill of you. But to be seen staring at a bird for five minutes ... or picking roadside weeds. ... It is fortunate there are asylums ... and who knows how soon he may become dangerous.

—Birds in the Bush

White-throats: Children of the Wilderness

White-throats are children of the wilderness. It is one charm of their music that it always comes, or seems to come, from such a distance—from far up the mountain side, or from the inaccessible depths of some ravine.

—Birds in the Bush

A Certain Accent

The veery's mood is not so lofty as the hermit's, nor is his music to be compared for brilliancy and fullness with that of the wood thrush; but more than any other bird known to me, the veery's has ... the accent of sanctity.

—Birds in the Bush

Goldfinch— Loveliest of Birds

Our American goldfinch is one of the loveliest of birds. With his elegant plumage, his rhythmical, undulatory flight, his beautiful song, and his more beautiful soul, he ought to be one of the best beloved. ...

—Birds in the Bush

The Commonness of Miracles

Everything is a miracle from somebody's point of view.

—Birds in the Bush

It is true of birds, as of men, that some have more individuality than others. But know any bird or any man well enough and he will prove to be himself and nobody else.

—*Birds in the Bush*

The Individuality of Birds and Men

The time will come, we … hope, when doctors will prescribe bird-gazing instead of blue-pill.

—*Birds in the Bush*

Bird-Watching for Health

I cannot recall that any one of my teachers ever called my attention to a natural object. It seems incredible, but … I was never in the habit of observing the return of the birds in the spring or their departure in autumn … but now … my ignorance was converted all at once into a kind of blessing … no sooner had I begun to read bird books and consult … mounted specimens, than every turn out-of-doors became full of … delightful surprises.

—*Birds in the Bush*

An Awakening

What we find in our friends depends in great part on what we have in ourselves.

—*Birds in the Bush*

What We Find in Our Friends

You hear a song in the village street and pass along unmoved; but stand in the silence of the forest, with your feet in a bed of creeping snowberry and oxalis, and the same song goes to your soul.

—*Birds in the Bush*

Time, Circumstance, and Bird Song

213

Improvement on a Custom of the Ancients

We have improved on the custom of the ancients: they examined a bird's entrails; we listen to his song.

—*Birds in the Bush*

Variations in a Bird's Song

It is an indiscretion ever to say of a bird that he has only such and such notes. You may have been his friend for years, but the next time you go into the woods he will likely enough put you to shame by singing something not so much as hinted at in your description.

—*Birds in the Bush*

The Eye Is a Window

Truly the human eye is nothing more than a window, of no use unless the man looks out of it.

—*Birds in the Bush*

Pursuing the Unattainable

Life would soon lose its charm for most of us ... if we could no longer pursue the unattainable.

—*Birds in the Bush*

To Have a Mystery

In this age, when the world is in such danger of becoming omniscient ... it is good to have here and there a mystery in reserve. Though it be only one, we may well cherish it as a treasure.

—*Birds in the Bush*

The Untrained Ear

There is nothing about the human ear more wonderful than its ability not to hear.

—*Birds in the Bush*

Others will discover in the birds ... many things that I miss, and perhaps will miss some things which I have treated. ... It remains only for each to testify what he has seen, and at the end to confess that a soul, even the soul of a bird, is after all a mystery.

—*Birds in the Bush*

The Undiscovered in Birds

It is with birds as with other poets: the smaller gift need not be the less genuine; and they whom the world calls greatest ... may possibly not be the ones who touch us most intimately, or to whom we return oftenest and with most delight.

—*Birds in the Bush*

The Minor Songsters

It is always a double pleasure to find a plodding, humdrum–seeming man with a poet's heart ... a little of the same delighted surprise is felt by everyone, I imagine, when he learns for the first time that our little brown creeper is a singer.

—*Birds in the Bush*

Our Surprising Brown Creeper

The goldfinch loses his bright feathers and canary-like song as the cold season approaches, but not even a New England winter can rob him of his sweet call and his cheerful spirit. ... I think him never more winsome than when he hangs ... above a snow-bank on a bleak January morning.

—*Birds in the Bush*

The Goldfinch in Winter

It is pleasant to observe how naturally birds flock together in hard times—precisely as men do, and doubtless for similar reasons.

—*Birds in the Bush*

Every bird's voice has something characteristic about it, just as every human voice has tones and inflections which those who are ... familiar with its owner, will infallibly detect.

—*Birds in the Bush*

Now I pass two long-armed white oaks, which I never come near without thinking of a friend of mine ... who used to walk hereabouts with me; a real tree lover, who loves not species, not white oaks, and red oaks, but individual trees, and goes to see them as one goes to see a man or a woman.

—*The Clerk of the Woods*

Distance softens sound as it softens the landscape, and as time, which is only another kind of distance, softens grief.

—*The Clerk of the Woods*

There is something in a boy's spirits that a man's money can never buy, nor a man's will bring back to him.

—*The Clerk of the Woods*

Mountains and trees make me humble. I feel like a poor relation.

—*The Clerk of the Woods*

Running water is one of the universal parables, appealing to something primitive and ineradicable in human nature. Day and night it preaches—sermons without words. It is every man's friend. The more stolid find it good company. For that reason, largely, men love to fish. They are poets without knowing it. They have never read a line of verse since they outgrew Mother Goose; they never consciously admire a landscape; they care nothing for a picture, unless it is a caricature, or tells a story; but they cannot cross moving water without feeling its charm.

—The Clerk of the Woods

The Charm of Running Water

Leaves are rustling below and above. As is true sometimes in higher circles, they seem to grow loquacious with age; the slightest occasion, the merest nudge of suggestion, the faintest puff of the spirit sets them off. For me they will never talk too much. I love their preaching seven days in the week. The driest of them never teased my ears with a dry sermon. I scuff along the path on purpose to stir them up. "Your turn will come next," I hear them saying; but the message does not sound like bad news. I listen to it with a kind of pleasure, as to solemn music. If the doctor or the clergyman had brought me the same word, my spirit might have risen in rebellion; but the falling leaf may say what it likes. It has poet's leave.

—The Clerk of the Woods

The Message of Talking Leaves

Every kind of bird has motions of its own, no doubt, if we look sharply enough.

—The Clerk of the Woods

A Bird's Motions

The Sweetest Music

There is no music sweeter than wood silence. ... It is not strictly silence, though it is what we call by that name. There is no song. No one speaks. The wind is not heard in the branches. But there is a nameless something in the air, an inaudible noise, or an audible stillness, of which you become conscious if you listen for it; a union of fine sounds ... distant crickets, few and faint, and a hum as of tiny wings. ...

—*The Clerk of the Woods*

What We Turn to Nature For

... Worldlings and matter-of-fact men do not know it, but what quiet nature lovers (not scenery hunting tourists) go to nature in search of is not the excitement of novelty, but a refreshment of the sensibilities. You may call it comfort, consolation, tranquillity, peace of mind, a vision of truth, an uplifting of the heart, a stillness of the soul, a quickening of the imagination, what you will. It is of different shades, and so may be named in different words. It is theirs who have the secret, and the rest would not divine your meaning though your speech were transparency itself.

To my thinking, no one, not even Thoreau, or Jefferies, or Wordsworth, ever said a truer word about it than Keats dropped in one of his letters. Nothing in his poems is more deeply poetical. "The setting sun will always set me to rights," he says, "or if a sparrow come before my window, I take part in his existence and pick about in the gravel." There you have the soul of the matter, "I take part in his existence." When you do that, the bird or the flower may be never so common or so humble. Your walk has prospered.

—*The Clerk of the Woods*

VAN DYKE, HENRY (1852–1933)

American clergyman, educator, novelist, essayist, poet and author

You never get so close to the birds as when you are wading quietly down a little river, ...
—*Little Rivers*

To Get Close to Birds

This is the true bird of the brook, after all, the winged spirit of cheerfulness and contentment, the patron saint of little rivers, the fisherman's friend.
—*Little Rivers*

Song Sparrow—The Fisherman's Friend

Every land has its nightingale, if we only have the heart to hear him.
—*Little Rivers*

Every Land Has Its Nightingale

There is a secret pleasure in finding these delicate flowers in the rough heart of the wilderness. It is like discovering the veins of poetry in the character of a guide or a lumberman.
—*Little Rivers*

Flowers in the Wilderness

The blueberry is nature's compensation for the ruin of forest fires. It grows best where the woods have been burned away and the soil is too poor to raise another crop of trees.
—*Little Rivers*

Blueberries and Forest Fires

Good Fellowship of a River

A river is the most human and companionable of all inanimate things. It has a life, a character, a voice of its own, and is as full of good fellowship as a sugar-maple is of sap. It can talk in various tones, loud or low, and of many subjects grave and gay. ... For real company and friendship, there is nothing outside of the animal kingdom that is comparable to a river.

—*Little Rivers*

The Sacrifice of Useless, "Pretty" Things

I fancy there are a good many people ... chopping down all the native growths of life, clearing the ground of all the useless pretty things that seem to cumber it, sacrificing everything to utility and success. We fell the last green tree for the sake of raising an extra hill of potatoes; and never stop to think what an ugly, barren place we may have to sit in while we eat them.

—*Little Rivers*

VERGIL (70–19 B.C.)
(PUBLIUS VERGILIUS MARO)
Roman poet and philosopher

The Woodland Gods

And happy he, who has knowledge of the woodland gods.

—*Georgics, ii, 493*

VOLTAIRE (1694–1778)
(FRANÇOIS MARIE AROUET)
French satirist, philosopher, historian, dramatist and poet

Faith consists in believing when it is beyond the power of reason to believe. It is not enough that a thing be possible for it to be believed.
—*The Oxford Dictionary of Quotations*

What Faith Is

WALLACE, DAVID RAINS (1945–)
American author, naturalist, evolutionist and teacher; recipient of the California's Commonwealth Club Silver medal for Literature and an Arts Literature Fellowship (1979); winner of the John Burroughs Medal for *The Klamath Knot* (1984)

Evolution is not only a battle of numbers wherein the fit survive and the rest get dragged out by the heels. There are other ways for life to evolve besides competition. The conventional Darwinian picture of an apparently peaceful landscape which underneath is a seething battle is after all a picture, an artifact imposed in physical reality. To the pre-Darwinian senses, a peaceful landscape is just that. Landscapes have evolved from cooperation among organisms as well as from competition. If it seems anthropomorphic to speak of the cooperation between trees and insects, is it any less so to speak of their competing?
—*The Klamath Knot*

Evolution

Land Animals

... we are land animals. The human mind is much more a product of forest shadows than of water's glitter. Perhaps this is what daunts us about forests that they are like us, secretive, labyrinthine. We have lived with forest trees for millions of years, yet how little we understand of them. We only very recently have realized that, in their way, they are as alive as we are. If their lives seem rudimentary and simple, this only reflects this rude simplicity of our knowledge. It would be a greater thing than talking to dolphins really to understand the slow life of a forest tree as it passes its millennium of steadfast silence. ...

—*The Klamath Knot*

WALTON, IZAAC (1593–1683)

English author, famous for his classic treatise on fishing, *The Compleat Angler*

The Nightingale's Heavenly Music

And I thought, too, of the nightingale, which breathes such sweet loud music out of her little instrumental throat that it might make mankind to think miracles are not ceased. He that at midnight ... should hear, as I have very often, the clear airs, the sweet descants, the natural rising and falling, the doubling and redoubling of her voice, might well be lifted above earth and say, "Lord, what music hast Thou provided for the saints in heaven, when Thou affordest bad men such music on earth."

—*The Compleat Angler*

... he that hopes to be a good angler must not only bring an inquiring, searching, observing wit, but he must also bring a large measure of hope and patience and a love and propensity for the art itself. But having once got and practiced it, then doubt not but angling will prove to be ... like virtue, a reward to itself.

—*The Compleat Angler*

To Be a Good Fisherman

... he that views the ancient Ecclesiastical Canons ... shall find Angling allowed to clergymen as being a harmless recreation, a recreation that invites them to contemplation and quietness.

—*The Compleat Angler*

The Rewards of Fishing

Money-getting men, men that spend all their time, first in getting, and next in anxious care to keep it; men that are condemned to be rich, and then always buy or are discontented; for these poor–rich men, we Anglers pity them perfectly, and stand in no need to borrow their thoughts to think ourselves so happy.

—*The Compleat Angler*

The Poor Rich-Men

Izaak believed that fish could hear; if they can, then their vocabulary must be full of strange oaths, for all anglers are not patient men.

—*The Compleat Angler*

*All Anglers Are
Not Patient Men*

Unless a man makes a fly to counterfeit that very fly in that place, he is like to lose his labour. ... Three or four flies neat and rightly made and not too big, serve for a Trout in most rivers, all the summer.

—*The Compleat Angler*

Recipe for Trout-fishing

No Man Born an Angler

As no man is born an artist, so no man is born an Angler

—*The Compleat Angler*

WATERTON, CHARLES (1782–1865)
British naturalist, explorer and writer, famous for his magnum opus, *Wanderings in South America*

Bird Voices in a Tropical Forest

He whose eye can distinguish the various beauties of uncultivated nature, and whose ear is not shut to the wild sounds in the woods, will be delighted in passing up the River Demerara [a river in Guyana]. Every now and then the maam or tinamou sends forth one long and plaintive whistle from the depth of the forest, and then stops; whilst the yelping of the toucan and the shrill voice of the bird called pi-pi-yo is heard during the interval. The campanero never fails to attract the attention of the passenger; at a distance of nearly three miles you may hear this snow-white bird tolling every four or five minutes, like the distant convent-bell. From six to nine in the morning the forests resound with the mingled cries and strains of the feathered race; after this they gradually die away. From eleven to three all nature is hushed as in a midnight silence, and scarce a note is heard, saving that of the campanero and the pi-pi-yo; it is then that, oppressed by the solar heat, the birds retire to the thickest shade and wait for the refreshing cool of evening. ...

—*Wanderings in South America*

The harmless, unoffending goat-sucker, from the time of Aristotle to the present day, has been in disgrace with man. Father has handed down to son, and author to author, that this nocturnal thief subsists by milking the flocks. Poor injured little bird of night, how sadly has thou suffered, and how foul a stain has inattention to facts put upon thy character! Thou hast never robbed many of any part of his property nor deprived the kid of a drop of milk.

When the moon shines bright ... you will see it close by the cows, goats and sheep, jumping up every now and then under their bellies. Approach a little nearer. ... See how the nocturnal flies are tormenting the herd, and with what dexterity he springs up and catches them as fast as they alight on the belly, legs and udder of the animals. Observe how quiet they stand, and how sensible they seem of his good offices, for they neither strike at him nor hit him with their tail, nor tread on him, nor try to drive him away as an uncivil intruder. Were you to dissect him, and inspect his stomach, you would find no milk there. It is full of flies which have been annoying the herd.

—*Wanderings in South America*

The Poor,
Maligned Goatsucker

WEEKS, EDWARD A. (1898–1989)
American editor and writer

The Immortal Trees

Of all growing things, a tree is the most nearly immortal. Seeing them unchanged year after year, gives us the illusion that we, ourselves, change little. To walk in this pine woods was to find tranquillity. ...These evenly spaced boles with their canopy meeting overhead stood for order and calm ... a small calm universe. All of us who walk for thought have our secret places. ... This was mine.

—*The Open Heart*

WHEELER, WILLIAM M. (1865–1937)
American entomologist and author

Insect Life

The activities of insects, like those of other animals, are an expression of three fundamental appetites. Two of these—hunger and sex—are positive and possessive, the other—fear or avoidance—is negative and avertive.

—*Social Life Among the Insects*

WHITE, GILBERT (1720–1793)

English clergyman, naturalist, author of books of natural history and founder of the naturalist school of close observation and analysis

The grasshopper-lark began his sibilous note in my fields last Saturday. Nothing can be more amusing than the whisper of this little bird, which seems to be close by though at a hundred yards distance; and when close at your ear, is scarce any louder than when a great way off. Had I not been a little acquainted with insects, and known that the grasshopper kind is not yet hatched, I should have hardly believed but that it had been a *locusta* whispering in the bushes.
—*The Natural History of Selborne*

The Amusing Song of the Grasshopper-Lark

When I used to rise in the morning last autumn, and see the swallows and martins clustering on the chimneys and thatch of the neighboring cottages, I could not help being touched with a secret delight, mixed with some degree of mortification: with delight, to observe with how much ardor and punctuality these poor little birds obeyed the strong impulse toward migration, ... and with some degree of mortification, when I reflected that, ... we are not yet quite certain to what regions they do migrate. ...
—*The Natural History of Selborne*

The Migration of Birds

The house-swallow washes by dropping into the water as it flies. ...
—*The Natural History of Selborne*

How the Swallow Bathes

Bird Song and Incubation

... I lay it down as a maxim in ornithology, that as long as there is any incubation going on there is music.

—*The Natural History of Selborne*

The Value of Softness in an Owl's Feathers

The plumage ... of the wings of every species of owl that I have yet examined is remarkably soft and pliant. Perhaps it may be necessary that the wings of these birds should not make much resistance or rushing, that they may ... steal through the air unheard upon a nimble and watchful quarry.

—*The Natural History of Selborne*

What a Good Ornithologist Should Know

A good ornithologist should be able to distinguish birds by their air as well as by their colours and shape; on the ground as well as on the wing: and in the bush as well as in the hand.

—*The Natural History of Selborne*

The Language of Birds

The language of birds is very ancient, and, like other ancient modes of speech, very elliptical; little is said, but much is meant and understood.

—*The Natural History of Selborne*

Facts About Birds Awaiting Discovery

It is now more than forty years that I have paid some attention to the ornithology of this district, without being able to exhaust the subject: new occurrences still arise as long as any inquiries are kept alive.

—*The Natural History of Selborne*

Birds that fly by night are obliged to be noisy; their notes, often repeated, become signals or watchwords to keep them together, that they may not stray or lose each other in the dark.
—*The Natural History of Selborne*

The Bird's Voice Is a Pilot

... the investigation of the life and conversation of animals is a concern of much more trouble and difficulty, and is not to be attained, but by the active and inquisitive, and by those that reside much in the country.
—*The Natural History of Selborne*

To Learn About Animals

The two great motives which regulate the proceedings of the brute creation are love and hunger; the former incites animals to perpetuate their kind; the latter induces them to preserve individuals. ...
—*The Natural History of Selborne*

Love and Hunger

Perseverance will accomplish anything. ...
—*The Natural History of Selborne*

Perseverance

The most insignificant insects and reptiles ... have much more influence in the economy of Nature, than the incurious are aware of; and are mighty in their effect, from their minuteness ... and fecundity.
—*The Natural History of Selborne*

The Importance of Small Animals

All nature is so full that that district produces the greatest variety which is the most examined.
—*The Natural History of Selborne*

The Fullness of Nature

How Bats Drink

Bats drink on the wing, like swallows, by sipping the surface, as they play over pools and streams. They love to frequent waters, not only for the sake of drinking, but on account of insects, which are found over them in the greatest plenty.

—*The Natural History of Selborne*

The Sociality of Animals

There is a wonderful spirit of sociality in the brute creation, independent of sexual attachment: the congregating of gregarious birds in the winter is a remarkable instance.

Many horses, though quiet with company, will not stay one minute in a field by themselves: the strongest fences cannot restrain them. Oxen and cows will not fatten by themselves. ... It would be needless to instance in sheep, which constantly flock together.

But this propensity seems not to be confined to animals of the same species; for we know a doe, still alive, that was brought up from a little fawn with a dairy of cows; with them it goes a-field, and with them it returns to the yard. The dogs of the house take no notice of the deer, being used to her; but, if strange dogs come by, a chase ensues; while the master smiles to see his favorite securely leading her pursuers over hedge, or gate, or stile, till she returns to the cows, who, with fierce lowing and menacing horns, drive the assailants quite out of the pasture.

Even great disparity of kind and size does not always prevent social advances and mutual fellowship. For a very intelligent and observant person has assured me that, ... keeping but one horse, he happened also on a time to have but one solitary hen. These two incongruous animals spent much of their time together in a lonely orchard, where they saw no creature but each other. By degrees an apparent regard began to take place between these two sequestered animals. The fowl would approach the quadruped with notes of complacency, rubbing herself gently against his legs; while the horse would look down with satisfaction, and move with the greatest caution and circumspection, lest he should trample on his diminutive companion. Thus, by mutual good offices, each seemed to console the vacant hours of the other.

—*The Natural History of Selborne*

To a thinking mind nothing is more wonderful than that early instinct which impresses young animals with a notion of the situation of their natural weapons, and of using them properly in their own defence, even before those weapons subsist or are formed. Thus a young cock will spar at his adversary before his spurs are grown; and a calf or a lamb will push with their heads before their horns are sprouted. In the same manner did these young adders attempt to bite before their fangs were in being.

—*The Natural History of Selborne*

Defenses of Young Animals

The natural term of a hog's life is little known, and the reason is plain—because it is neither profitable nor convenient to keep that turbulent animal to the full extent of its time. ...

—*The Natural History of Selborne*

The Length of a Hog's Life

Ever-fresh Beauty of Sussex Downs

Though I have now travelled the Sussex Downs upwards of thirty years, yet I still investigate that chain of majestic mountains with fresh admiration year by year; and I think I see new beauties every time I traverse it.

—The Natural History of Selborne

Echoes

In a district so diversified as this, so full of hollow vales and hanging woods, it is no wonder that echoes should abound. Many we have discovered that return the cry of a pack of dogs, the notes of a hunting horn, a tunable ring of bells, or the melody of birds. ... All echoes have some one place to which they are returned stronger and more distinct than to any other; and that is always the place that lies at right angles with the object of repercussion, and is not too near, not too far off.

—The Natural History of Selborne

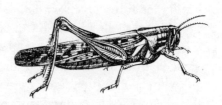

The Shrilling of the Field Cricket

Sounds do not always give us pleasure according to their sweetness and melody; nor do harsh sounds always displease. Thus the shrilling of the field-cricket, though sharp and stridulous, yet marvellously delights some hearers, filling their minds with ... everything that is rural, verdurous, and joyous.

—The Natural History of Selborne

WHITMAN, WALT(ER) (1819–1892)
American poet, journalist and essayist

Urge and urge and urge,
Always the procreant urge of the world:
Out of the dimness opposite equals
    advance, always substance and
    increase, alway sex,
Always a knit of identity, always
    distinction, always a breed of life.
          —*Song of Myself, Leaves of Grass*

The Procreant Urge

Oxen that rattle the yoke and chain or
    halt in the leafy shade, what is
that you express in your eyes
It seems to me more than all the print I
    have read in my life.
          —*Song of Myself, Leaves of Grass*

Oxen That
Rattle the Yoke

My tread scares the wood–drake and wood–duck
on my distant and day–long ramble,
They rise together, they slowly circle around.

I believe in those wing'd purposes,
And do not call the tortoise unworthy
because she is not something else …
          —*Song of Myself, Leaves of Grass*

Departures

Miracles

I believe a leaf of grass is no less than
    the journey–work of the stars,
And the pismire is equally perfect, and
    a grain of sand, and the egg of the wren,
And the tree-toad is a chef-d'oeuvre for
    the highest,
And the running blackberry would
    adorn the parlors of heaven
And the narrowest hinge in my hand
    puts to scorn all machinery,
And the cow crunching with depress'd
    head surpasses any statue,
And a mouse is miracle enough to
    stagger sextillions of infidels.

          —*Song of Myself, Leaves of Grass*

The Animals

I think I could turn and live with
    animals, they're so placid and self-contain'd,
I stand and look at them long and long.

They do not sweat and whine about
    their condition,
They do not lie awake in the dark and
    weep for their sins,
They do not make me sick discussing
    their duty to God,
Not one is dissatisfied, not one is
    demented with the mania of owning
    things,
Not one kneels to another, nor to his
    kind that lived thousands of years ago,
Not one is respectable or unhappy over
    the whole earth.

          —*Song of Myself, Leaves of Grass*

The long brown path before me leading
wherever I choose.
> —*Song of the Open Road,*
> *Leaves of Grass*

Prospects

Out of the mockingbird's throat, the
musical shuttle ...
> —*Out of the Cradle Endlessly Rocking,*
> *Leaves of Grass*

Mockingbird Music

WILLIAMS, TENNESSEE (1914–1983)
(PEN NAME OF THOMAS LANIER WILLIAMS)
American playwright and fiction writer

... among the unsophisticated, there still
exists a conspiracy to destroy the sensitive
people of the earth.
> —*Quoted in* Esquire, *September 1971*

Plight of the Sensitive

WILLIAMSON, HENRY (1897–1977)
English novelist and nature writer

No beauty remains inviolate for long.
> —*The Lone Swallows*

Beauty

The sweet little whispering call of my
longtailed titmice fashioning their bottle nest,
so happy in the sunshine, is a wider and more
profound utterance than all the philosophy
collected from the books of the world. ...
> —*The Lone Swallows*

*The Enduring
Wisdom of Birds*

The Swift— Mystic Among Birds

The swift is the mystic among birds. He is aloof from other birds—apart from life. He is never seen to perch unless it be on the rigging of a ship during migration. The swift is black, he screams shrilly as he darts through the air, his wings are curved like a boomerang. During June I have seen and heard them long after midnight, whole cohorts of them wheeling in the sky, their cries sounding like the thin jingle of a frail chain.

—The Lone Swallows

Love-chase of the Peregrines

Swiftly and with quick wing-beats the peregrines climb, almost vertically. Then a sudden speeding at eighty or ninety miles an hour, a downward dash at the rocks, beaks and wings touching; they hiss past the gulls, swoop apart and glide upwards, uttering their sweetly wild mating cries. Nothing matters in the ecstasies of spring. They may pass uncaring within a few yards of the beholder, when he may see the neck and wings, slate-ash in colour, the dark crown and nape, the hooked beak and the barred tail. He may shout and wave his arms in excitement, the ravens croak, the gulls scream, the lone buzzard wail as he circles, but the love-chase continues. On the falcons rush, above the crested waves and the marble troughs of the ocean, past the crannies and the ledges of the precipice, among the summer cloudlets, over the hills of heather and the slopes of golden gorse, by the mounded sand-dunes, and the glistening mud-flats; all the heavenly freeness is theirs to roam.

—The Lone Swallows

The little spider paused half-way between the leaves. Perhaps some flaw in his architectural home was apparent to him, or he feared that the wind of the summer night would destroy his foundation threads. Born only a few weeks before, without tuition or practice, he knew the angles of his pillars, the proportions of his stanchions, the symmetry and balance of his walls. He had watched no honey-coloured parent at work, yet within his minute brain were the plans of a perfect system to entangle the smallest flying insects, feeble of wing, that would fall against his web. ...The spider moved on as the first star shone in the sky. Gradually the sun sank into the sea, ... an owl quavered in loneliness as it fanned over the churchyard; a jackdaw answered sharply, querulously, and night had come to the earth.

—*The Lone Swallows*

The Knowingness of the Spider

The Lapwing's Secret

... the lapwing holds the secret of the swamps and boglands, and you hear it in his wild voice as his wings sough above. In the early spring he makes over the dull furrows his plaintive music, climbing high and diving to the ground as though it were sweet ecstasy to fall, wing-crumpled and broken-hearted, before his mate.

—*The Lone Swallows*

The Robin's Immortal Life

... Somewhere a robin was singing. He did not need to brood upon immortality—he lives unconscious of time ... the beauty of the earth and the sun, and his mate, all accepted without question. The robin lives like an immortal here, upon the earth that is so beautiful; and all the wisdom of the dead civilisations is nothing to what the robin's song tells, if you will but listen.

—*The Lone Swallows*

The Need for an Open Mind

The more one thinks one knows of nature the more open should be the mind. ...

—*The Lone Swallows*

Summer Without Dandelions

Summer to me would be incomplete without the dandelions. For what they symbol, would that there were more in the drifted dust of the cities.

—*The Lone Swallows*

The Lure of the Great Cities

The old spirit of the country is dying, and the factory and town calls to its children—there is more life there, and more money to be made.

—*The Lone Swallows*

WILSON, ALEXANDER (1766–1813)

Scottish immigrant, pioneering American ornithologist, bird artist and distinguished and accurate observer; author of eight-volume *American Ornithology* (1808–1814), illustrated with his paintings and drawings of 262 species of American birds; called the Father of American Ornithology

The Heart and Purpose of Alexander Wilson

March 31, 1804

... I was always an enthusiast in my admiration of the rural scenery of Nature, but since your example and encouragement have set me to attempt to imitate her productions, I see new beauties in every bird, plant or flower. ...

I sometimes smile to think that while others are immersed in deep schemes of speculation and aggrandizement—in building towns and purchasing plantations, I am entranced in contemplation over the plumage of a lark, or gazing like a despairing lover, on the lineaments of an owl. While others are hoarding up their bags of money, without the power of enjoying it, I am collecting, without injuring my conscience, or wounding my peace of mind, those beautiful specimens of Nature's works that are ever pleasing. I have had live crows, hawks and owls, opossums, squirrels, snakes, lizards, etc. so that my room has sometimes reminded me of Noah's ark. ... A boy not long ago brought me a large basket full of crows. ...One boy caught a mouse in school, ... I set about drawing it that same evening, and all the while the pantings of its little heart showed it to be in the most extreme agonies of fear. I had intended to kill it, in order to fix it in the claws of a stuffed owl, but happening to spill a few drops of water near where it was tied, it lapped it up with such eagerness, and looked in my face with such an eye of supplicating terror, as perfectly overcame me. I immediately untied it and restored it to life and liberty. The agonies of a prisoner at the stake, while the fire and instruments of torment are preparing, could not be more severe than the sufferings of that poor mouse; and, insignificant as the object was, I felt at that moment the sweet sensations that mercy leaves on the mind when she triumphs over cruelty.

—*Letter to William Bartram, American Ornithology or the Natural History of the Birds in the United States*

The Eternal Song

Bury me where the birds will sing over my grave.

—*The American Treasury*

WILSON, WOODROW (1856–1924)
Twenty-eighth president of the United States, scholar, champion of world peace and democracy and president of Princeton University (1902–1910)

Why You Are Here

You are here in order to enable the world to live more amply, with greater vision, with a finer spirit of hope and achievement. You are here to enrich the world, and you impoverish yourself if you forget the errand.

YUTANG, LIN (1895–1976)
Chinese teacher, translator, editor and writer

Religion by the Back Door

I do not think it is important whether a man enters religion by the front door or the back door, as long as he enters. For only as he enters does he find peace. If to find God by the garden path is the back door, then by all means go down the garden path. We have no approach to heaven save by the lower senses, and so far the back door to religion seems the safest. If we can arrive at a position in which Jesus admired the lilies of the valley and St. Francis loved the birds as God's own creatures, we have stumbled upon the very source from which all religions took their rise. ...

—*On The Wisdom of America*

When one's senses are fully awakened ...
the true feast is neither food nor wine, nor the
salutary aroma of tobacco, but nature itself.
Only people who live on cement streets and
carpeted floors can ever forget the inherent
drama in nature and, by mere habits of city
living, become nature–blind.
> —*On the Wisdom of America*

Nature—The True Feast

There is no value in life except what you
choose to place upon it, and no happiness in
any place except what you bring to it yourself.
> —*On the Wisdom of America*

*What We Get
from Life is Ourselves*

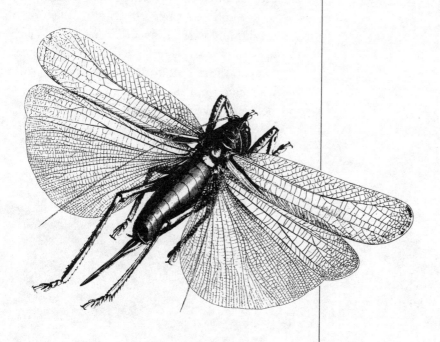

ZWINGER, ANN (1925–)

American writer, artist and instructor in art and art history; received an Indiana author's Day Award (1971) for nature and ecology writing and a National Book Award nomination (1972); winner of the John Burroughs Medal for *Run, River, Run* (1976)

Gray Rock Canyon at Dawn

I lie awake most of the night, sensitized to the river. Peace, contentment: these are programmed cultural words; what I feel is the infinity outside of culture, and although I sleep little, I awake rested. The dawn sky is pale and pearly, like a moonstone, webbed with a few clouds, the jagged skyline just beginning to pick up sunlight, that beautiful moment before full awakening when the world is fresh and clear and all is possible and good, a time of great expectations, and it is completely right, this gray rock canyon, this cold rock beginning this beautiful river morning.

—*Run, River, Run*

The river becomes a way of thinking, ingrained, a way of looking at the world. I listen to its commentary on the rocks and willows that block its way, feel cooled by the touch of spray, and smell all the odors that emanate from it. Judgment and recognition of odors depend so much on familiar reference smells that it is difficult to describe a new smell without recourse to them. The river, of course, often smells of off-river odors: the sweet, heavy aroma of an acre of sand verbena, a dead cow on a gravel bar, wet stones, cold muck. But it also smells of itself, an aloof and elusive smell, soft, faintly like clean clay or like wet wash hanging out on a windy day. It is neither sweet nor sharp, acrid nor aromatic, nor distinctly anything ever smelled before or elsewhere unless one has had a river in his or her childhood. It is a smooth, tentative smell. It is light and deep, cool, it comes in curling tendrils and sometimes it is difficult to pick out from other smells. But it is there. And, once smelled, it becomes easier to recognize and soon there is almost a sense of river in the landscape even when it cannot be seen.

—*Run, River, Run*

The Elusive Smell of the River

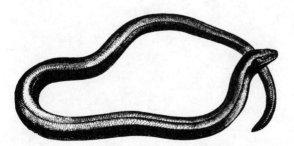

Evans, Howard S. Reproduced by permission of the Smithsonian Institution Press from *Pleasures of Entomology: Portraits of Insects and the People Who Study Them*, Howard S. Evans. Copyright © Smithsonian Institution, Washington, D.C., 1985.

Halle, Louis J. *Birds Against Men*. The Viking Press, New York, 1938. Reprinted by permission of Penguin USA, New York.

Kieran, John. *Footnotes on Nature*. Copyright © 1947. Permission granted by Doubleday, a division of Bantam, Doubleday, Dell Publishing Group, Inc., New York.

Krutch, Joseph Wood. Excerpts from *The Great Chain Of Life*. Copyright © 1956 by Joseph Wood Krutch. Copyright © renewed 1984 by Marcelle L. Krutch. Reprinted by permission of Houghton Mifflin Co., Boston.

Lawrence, Louise de Kiriline. *The Lovely and the Wild*. Copyright © 1962. McGraw-Hill, Inc. Reprinted by permission of McGraw-Hill, Inc., New York.

Leopold, Aldo. From *A Sand County Almanac, With Other Essays on Conservation from Round River* by Aldo Leopold. Copyright © 1949, 1953, 1966, renewed 1977, 1981 by Oxford University Press, Inc., New York. Reprinted by permission.

Longstreth, T. Morris. From *Knowing the Weather* by T. Morris Longstreth. Copyright © 1953 by T. Morris Longstreth. Reprinted with permission of Macmillan Publishing Company, New York.

Lopez, Barry Holstun. From *Arctic Dreams* by Barry Lopez. Copyright © 1986 Barry Holstun Lopez. Reprinted by permission of Charles Scribner's Sons, an imprint of Macmillan Publishing Company, New York.

Lopez, Barry Holstun. From *Wolves and Men* by Barry Lopez. Copyright © 1978 Barry Holstun Lopez. Reprinted by permission of Charles Scribner's Sons, an imprint of Macmillan Publishing Company.

Lorenz, Konrad Z. From *King Solomon's Ring* by Konrad Z. Lorenz. Copyright © 1952 by Konrad Z. Lorenz. Reprinted by permission of Harper & Row, Publishers, Inc., New York.

Matthiessen, Peter. *The Wind Birds*. The Viking Press, New York, 1967. Reprinted with permission of Penguin USA, New York.

Matthiessen, Peter. *Sand Rivers*. The Viking Press, New York, 1981. Reprinted with permission of Penguin USA, New York.

Milne, Lorus J. and Margery. Reprinted with permission of Atheneum Publishers, an imprint of Macmillan Publishing Company from *The Senses of Animals and Men* by Lorus J. and Margery Milne. Copyright © 1962 by Lorus J. Milne and Margery Milne.

Olson, Sigurd F. From *Open Horizons* by Sigurd F. Olson. Copyright © 1969 by Sigurd F. Olson. Reprinted by permission of Alfred A. Knopf, Inc., New York.

Olson, Sigurd F. *Wilderness Days* by Sigurd F. Olson. Copyright © 1972 by Sigurd F. Olson. Reprinted by permission of Alfred A. Knopf, Inc., New York.

Peattie, Donald C. *An Almanac for Moderns*. Published by G. P. Putnam's Sons. Copyright © 1935, 1963 by Donald C. Peattie. Reprinted by permission of Curtis Brown Ltd., New York.

Shapley, Harlow. From *A Treasury of Science* by Harlow Shapley, Samuel Rapport and Helen Wright. Copyright © 1958 by Harper & Row, Publishers, Inc., New York.

Skutch, Alexander Frank. *Nature Through Tropical Windows*. Copyright © 1983. Reprinted by permission of The University of California and the University of California Press.

Stanwell-Fletcher, Theodora. From *Driftwood Valley* by Theodora Stanwell-Fletcher. Copyright © 1946 by Theodora C. Stanwell-Fletcher. Reprinted by permission of Little, Brown and Company, Boston.

Stephens, James. From *Collected Poems*. Reprinted with permission of Macmillan Publishing Company. Copyright © 1926 by Macmillan Publishing Company, renewed 1954 by Cynthia Stephens.

Teal, John M. and Mildred M. *The Sargasso Sea*. Little, Brown and Company, Boston. Copyright © 1975. Reprinted by courtesy of John M. Teal and Mildred M. Teal.

Zwinger, Ann. *Run, River, Run*. Harper & Row. Reprinted by permission of Frances Collin, Agent, New York. Copyright © 1975 by Ann Zwinger.

BIBLIOGRAPHY

Abbey, Edward. *Desert Solitaire*. New York: McGraw-Hill Publishing Co., 1968.

Abbott, Charles C. *Days Out of Doors*. New York: D. Appleton and Co., 1889.

Adams, J. Donald. "Speaking of Books and Life." *New York Times Book Review Section*, February 8, 1953.

Alexander, Cecil Frances. *All Things Bright and Beautiful*. New York: Charles Scribner's Sons, 1962.

Aristotle. *Nichomachean Ethics*. Salem, N.H.: Ayer Co. Pubs., Rep. of 1909 ed.

Audubon, John James. *The Birds of America..* New York: Macmillan & Co., 1985.

Audubon, Maria. *Vol. I, Audubon and His Journals*. New York: Dover Publications, 1960.

Bartholin, Thomas. *New York Times Book Review*.

Bartram, William. *The Travels of William Bartram*. New York: Dover Publications,1928.

Bates, Henry. *The Naturalist on the River Amazons*. New York: D. Appleton Co., 1892.

Bates, Marston. *The Nature of Natural History*. New York: Macmillan Publishing Company, 1950.

Beebe, Charles William. *The Bird: Its Form and Function*. New York: Henry Holt & Co., 1906.

Beebe, Charles William. *Galapagos: World's End..* New York: G. P. Putnam's Sons, 1924.

Beebe, Charles William. *Jungle Days*. New York: G. P. Putnam's Sons, The Putnam Publishing Group, 1925.

Beebe, Charles William. *High Jungle*. New York: Duell, Sloan & Pearce, 1949.

Beebe, Charles William. *Log of the Sun*. New York: Henry Holt & Co., 1906.

Beebe, Charles William. *Nonsuch: Land of Water*. New York: Brewer, Warren & Putnam, 1932.

Belt, Thomas. *Introduction to the Naturalist in Nicaragua*. New York: Everyman's Library, E. P. Dutton Co., 1928.

Beston, Henry. *The Outermost House: A Year of Life on the Great Beach of Cape Cod*. Garden City, New York: Doubleday, Doran & Co., Inc., 1928.

Blake, William. *The Poems of William Blake*. Cambridge: Harvard University Press, 1969.

Blanton, Smiley. *Love or Perish*. New York: Simon & Schuster, 1956.

Bolles, Frank. *At the North of Bearcamp Water*. Cambridge,: The Riverside Press, Houghton Mifflin Co., 1893.

Borland, Hal. *Book of Days*. New York: Alfred A. Knopf, Inc., 1976.

Browne, Sir Thomas. *Religio Medici in Literary Masters of England*. New York: Rinehart & Company, Inc., 1936.

Browning, Robert. *Robert Browning's Poetry*. New York: W. W. Norton & Co., 1979.

Burgess, Anthony. *Modern Novels: The 99 Best. The New York Times*. February 5, 1984.

Burnford, Sheila. *One Woman's Arctic*. Boston: Little, Brown & Co., 1972.

Burroughs, John. Introduction to *Bird Neighbors* by Neltje Blanchan. Garden City, New York: Doubleday, Page and Company, 1922.

Burroughs, John. "In Warbler Time" published in *Bird–Lore Magazine*, February, 1899.

Burroughs, John. *The Heart of John Burroughs Journal*. Boston: Houghton Mifflin Co., 1956.

Burroughs, John. *Wake-Robin*. New York: William H. Wise Co., 1913.

Christensen, Clyde. *The Molds and Man: An Introduction to the Fungi*. Minneapolis: University of Minnesota Press, 1951.

Churchill, Sir Winston. *Nature Interlude, A Book of Natural History Quotations*. Compiled by E. F. Linssen, London: Williams & Norgate, Ltd., 1951.

Coman, Dale Rex. *The Endless Adventure*. Chicago: Henry Regnery Co., 1972.

Cott, Hugh B. *Adaptive Coloration in Animals*. Oxford, England: Oxford University Press, 1941.

Coues, Elliott. *Key to North American Birds*. Boston: The Page Company, 1903.

Cowper, William. *The Poetical Works of William Cowper*. Boston: The Athenaeum Press, 1898.

Darwin, Charles Robert. *The Origin of Species*. London: J. M. Dent & Sons, 1972.

Davis, Henry E. *The American Wild Turkey*. Georgetown, S.C.: Small Arms Technical Publishing Co., 1949.

Davis, William T. *Days Afield on Staten Island*. New York: Staten Island Historical Society, 1937.

Day, Clarence Shepard. *This Simian World*. New York: Alfred A. Knopf, Inc., 1968.

De la Mare, Walter. *The Collected Poems of Walter De la Mare*. London: Faber & Faber Ltd., 1979.

De Morgan, Augustus. *A Budget of Paradoxes*. Chicago: The Open Court Publishing Company, 1915.

Devoe, Alan. *Lives Around Us*. Creative Age Press, 1942.

Dickinson, Emily. *Final Harvest. Emily Dickinson's Poems*. Boston: Little, Brown & Company, 1961.

Dillard, Annie. *An American Childhood*. New York: Harper & Row, Publishers, Inc., 1987.

Dillard, Annie. *Pilgrim at Tinker Creek*. New York: Harper & Row, Publishers, Inc., 1974.

Dimnet, Ernest. *The Art of Thinking*. New York: Simon & Schuster, 1956.

Dobie, J. Frank. *The Voice of the Coyote*. Boston: Little, Brown and Co., 1947.

Donne, John. *Satyre, III, Complete Poetry and Selected Prose*. Edited by John Hayward. Bloomsbury, England: Nonesuch Press Ltd., 1929.

Edman, Irwin. *Under Whatever Sky*. New York: The Viking Press, 1951.

Edman, Irwin. *Adams: The Baby and the Man From Mars*. Quoted by Lin Yutang in *On the Wisdom of America*. New York: The John Day Co., 1960.

Edwards, Jonathan. *The New Dictionary of Thoughts*. Standard Book Company, 1961.

Eiseley, Loren. *The Lost Notebooks of Loren Eiseley*. Boston: Little, Brown and Company, 1987.

Ellwanger, George H. *The Natural History of Selborne*. by Gilbert White. New York: D. Appleton and Co., 1898

Emerson, Ralph Waldo. *Conduct of Life*. Boston: J. R. Osgood & Co., 1873.

Emerson, Ralph Waldo. *Emerson's Essays*. New York: Thomas Y. Crowell Company, 1926.

Emerson, Ralph Waldo. *Lectures and Biographical Sketches*. Boston: Riverside Press Edition, Houghton Mifflin Co., 1888.

Emerson, Ralph Waldo. *Letters and Social Aims.*Cambridge, Mass.: Riverside Press, Houghton Mifflin Co., 1904.

Emerson, Ralph Waldo. *Literary Ethics*. Boston and Cambridge: The Riverside Press, Houghton Mifflin Co.,

Emerson, Ralph Waldo. *Nature Addresses and Lectures*. Boston and Cambridge: Riverside Press Edition, Houghton Mifflin Co., 1903.

Emerson, Ralph Waldo. *Representative Men—Seven Lectures by Ralph Waldo Emerson*. New York: Hurst & Company, 1939.

Emerson, Ralph Waldo. *Society and Solitude*. Boston and Cambridge: The Riverside Press, Houghton Mifflin Co., 1904.

Emerson, Ralph Waldo. *The Complete Works of Ralph Waldo Emerson*. Boston and Cambridge: The Riverside Pocket Edition, 1876.

Emerson, Ralph Waldo. *The Early Lectures of Ralph Waldo Emerson*. Cambridge: Harvard University Press, 1962.

Evans, Howard S. *The Pleasures of Entomology: Portraits of Insects and the People Who Study Them*. Howard S. Evans. Smithsonian Institution, Washington, D.C. 1985.

Fabre, Jean Henri. *The Wonders of Instinct*. New York: The Century Company, 1918.

Fabre, Jean Henri. *Insect Adventures*. New York: Dodd, Mead and Company, 1932.

Fadiman, Clifton. "Boredom, Brainstorms and Bombs," *The Saturday Review of Literature*, August 31, 1957.

Fisher, James. *The Shell Bird Book*. London: Ebury Press and Michael Joseph, 1966.

Fisher, James and Roger Tory Peterson. *The World of Birds*. New York: Doubleday and Company, 1964.

Flagler, Henry Morrison. *The World of The Great White Heron* by Marjory Bartlett Sanger. New York: The Devin-Adair Co., 1967.

Gary, Romain. *A Love Letter to an Old Companion*. *Life Magazine*, "The Wild World," December 22, 1967.

Gay, John. *The Fables of John Gay*. London: Frederick Warne & Company, 1889.

Grey, Edward (Viscount Grey of Fallodon). *The Charm of Birds*. London: Hodder and Stoughton, 1927.

Halle, Jr., Louis J. *Birds Against Men*. New York: The Viking Press, 1938.

Harris, Sydney J. *Look Magazine*. April 29, 1958.

Heinrich, Bernd. *One Man's Owl*. Princeton, New Jersey: Princeton University Press, 1987.

Hoagland, Edward. In a review of *Black Sun* by Edward Abbey. *New York Times Sunday Book Review*, June 13, 1971.

Hubbard, Harlan. *Payne Hollow*. New York: The Eakins Press, 1974.

Hudson, William Henry. *Adventures Among Birds*. New York: Mitchell Kennerley Co., 1915.

Hudson, William Henry. *Birds in Town and Village*. New York: E. P. Dutton & Company, 1920.

Hudson, William Henry. *The Book of a Naturalist*. New York: George H. Doran Company, 1919.

Huxley, Julian. *Evolution in Action*. New York: Harper and Brothers, 1953.

Huxley, Thomas H. In *Life and Letters of Thomas H. Huxley* by Leonard Huxley. New York: D. Appleton and Company, 1901.

Jackson, Holbrook. *The Reading of Books*. New York: Charles Scribners' Sons, 1947.

Jefferies, Richard. *The Life of the Fields*. Edinburgh: Ballantyne, Hanson & Company, 1907.

Keats, John. *Letters of John Keats to His Family and Friends*. London: Macmillan & Co., 1921.

Kempis, Thomas à. (Thomas Hamerken von Kempen). Quoted by Hugh B. Cott in his preface to Adaptive Coloration of Animals. London: Methuen and Co. Ltd., 1941.

Kieran, John. *Footnotes on Nature*. New York: Doubleday Publishing Co., 1947.

Kilham, Lawrence. *On Watching Birds*. Chelsea, Vermont: Chelsea Green Publishing Company, 1988.

Kipling, Rudyard. *Just So Stories*. Mattituck, N.Y.: Amereon Ltd., 1976.

Krutch, Joseph Wood. *The Best of Two Worlds*. New York: William Sloane Associates, 1950.

Krutch, Joseph Wood. *The Desert Year*. New York: William Sloan Associates, 1951.

Krutch, Joseph Wood. *The Great Chain of Life*. Boston: Houghton Mifflin Co., 1956.

Landis, Paul. *Introduction to the Modern Library Edition of Four Famous Greek Plays*. New York: The Modern Library, Inc., 1929.

Lawrence, Louise De Kiriline. *The Lovely and The Wild*. New York: McGraw-Hill Publishing Company, 1962.

Le Gallienne, Richard. *The Lonely Dancers and Other Poems*. New York: John Lane Company, 1913.

Leopold, Aldo. *A Sand County Almanac*. New York: Oxford University Press, 1949.

Leopold, Aldo. *Round River*. New York: Oxford University Press, 1953.

Longfellow, Henry W. *The Sermon of St. Francis*. Garden City, New York: *Bartlett's Familiar Quotations*, Garden City Publishing Company, 1944.

Longstreth, T. Morris, *Knowing the Weather*. New York: Macmillan Publishing Company, 1943.

Lopez, Barry. *Arctic Dreams*. New York: Charles Scribner's Sons, 1986.

Lopez, Barry. *Of Wolves and Men*. New York: Macmillan Publishing Company, 1979.

Lorenz, Konrad Z. *King Solomon's Ring; New Light on Animal Ways*. New York: Harper & Row, Inc., 1952.

Lorenz, Konrad Z. *Man Meets Dog*. Baltimore, Md.: Penguin Books, 1953.

Lucretius. *Of the Nature of Things*. Cambridge: Everyman's Library.

Macleod, Fiona. *Where the Forest Murmurs*. New York: Charles Scribner's Sons, 1906.

Maeterlinck, Maurice. *The Life of the Bee*. New York: Dodd, Mead & Company, 1913.

Marcus Aurelius. *Meditations*. New York: Penguin Books, 1964.

Masefield, John. quoting *The Best Advice I Ever Had* by Unknown Author. *Saturday Review of Literature*, March 20, 1954.

Matthiessen, Peter. *The Wind Birds*. New York: The Viking Press, 1967.

Matthiessen, Peter. *Sand Rivers*. New York: The Viking Press, 1981.

Mills, Enos Abijah. *Wildlife On the Rockies*. Boston: Riverside Press, Houghton Mifflin Company, 1909.

Milne, Lorus J. and Margery. *The Senses of Animals and Men*. New York: Macmillan Publishing Company, 1962.

Momaday, N. Scott. *Words in the Blood: Contemporary Indian Writers of North and South America*. New York: New Library, 1984.

Montaigne, Michel de. *The Essays of Michel de Montaigne*. New York: The Heritage Press, 1946.

Muir, John. *A Thousand Mile Walk to the Gulf*. New York: The Riverside Press, Houghton Mifflin Company, 1916.

Murphy, Robert Cushman. *Logbook for Grace*. New York: Macmillan Company, 1950.

Olson, Sigurd F. *Open Horizons*. New York: Alfred A. Knopf, Inc., 1969.

Olson, Sigurd F. *Wilderness Days*. New York: Alfred A. Knopf, Inc., 1972.

Paton, Alan. Interview in *New York Times*, December 23, 1969.

Peattie, Donald C. *An Almanac for Moderns*. New York, G. P. Putnam's Sons, 1935.

Peattie, Donald C. *Audubon's America*. Boston: Houghton Mifflin Co., 1940.

Peterson, Roger Tory. *Birds Over America*. New York: Dodd, Mead & Co., 1948.

Rickett, Harold William. *The Green Earth, An Invitation to Botany*. New York: R. R. Bowker, Div. of Reed Publishing, 1943.

Roosevelt, Theodore. *A Book-Lover's Holidays in the Open*. New York: Charles Scribner's Sons, 1916.

Sa'di. *Tales from the Gulistan*. London: Philip Allan and Co., 1928.

Sass, Herbert Ravenel. *On the Wings of a Bird*. Garden City, N.Y.: Doubleday, Doran and Co., 1929.

Sass, Herbert Ravenel. *Adventures in Green Places*. New York: Minton, Balch & Co., 1926.

Schopenhauer, Arthur. *The Complete Essays*. New York: Willey Book Company, 1942.

Schopenhauer, Arthur. "Psychological Observations" from *Book III, Religion: A Dialogue*. New York: Willey Book Company, 1942.

Schweitzer, Albert. "The World of Albert Schweitzer." *The Saturday Review of Literature*, 1955.

Schweitzer, Albert. *The Animal World of Albert Schweitzer*. Boston: The Beacon Press, 1951.

Sears, Paul B. *Conservation, Please*. Pamphlet issued by The Women's Garden Clubs of America.

Shakespeare, William. *Measure for Measure*. New Haven, Conn.: Yale University Press, 1954.

Shakespeare, William. *Antony and Cleopatra*. Cambridge, Mass.: Harvard University Press, 1954.

Shapley, Harlow, Rapport, Samuel and Wright, Helen. *A Treasury of Science*. New York: Harper & Row Publishers, Inc., 1958.

Sharp, Dallas Lore. *A Watcher in the Woods*. New York: The Century Co., 1903.

Sharp, Dallas Lore. *Roof and Meadow*. New York: The Century Co., 1904.

Sharp, Dallas Lore. *Winter*. Boston: Houghton Mifflin Co., 1912.

Skutch, Alexander Frank. *Nature Through Tropical Windows*. Berkeley, Calif.: The University of California Press, 1983.

Stanhope, Philip Dormer (4th Earl of Chesterfield). *Lord Chesterfield's Letters to His Son*. Washington/London: M. W. Dunne, 1901.

Stanwell-Fletcher, Theodora. *Driftwood Valley*. Boston: Little, Brown and Company, 1946.

Steinhart, Peter. *The Meaning of Creeks*. Audubon magazine, May, 1989.

Stephens, James. *James Stephens Collected Poems*. New York: Macmillan Company, 1954.

Stringer, Arthur. *New York Times*. October 29, 1947.

Sutras. *Sutra-Kritanga Sutra*. 1:11:33, *New York Times Magazine*, February 19, 1956.

Sutton, George M. *Birds in the Wilderness*. New York: The Macmillan Co., 1936.

Taylor, Walter P. "Is Biology Obsolete?" *A.I.B.S. Bulletin*, June 1958.

Teal, John M. and Mildred M. *The Sargasso Sea*. Boston: Little, Brown and Company, 1975.

Teale, Edwin Way. *Near Horizons*. New York: Dodd, Mead & Co., 1942.

Tennyson, Alfred Lord. *The Complete Poetic Works of Tennyson*. Boston: Houghton Mifflin Company, 1898.

Thompson, Francis. *The Mistress of Vision*. Ditchling, Sussex, England: Douglas Pepler Co., 1918.

Thoreau, Henry David. *Autumn*. Boston: Houghton Mifflin Co., 1892.

Thoreau, Henry David. "Chesuncook." *The Atlantic Monthly*, 1858.

Thoreau, Henry David. *Early Spring in Massachusetts*. Cambridge: Houghton Mifflin Co., The Riverside Press, 1882

Thoreau, Henry David. *The Journal of Henry David Thoreau*. Edited by H. G. O. Blake, Cambridge: Houghton Mifflin Co., Riverside Press, 1887.

Thoreau, Henry David. *Walden*. New York: Walter J. Black Co., 1942.

Torrey, Bradford. *Birds in the Bush*. Boston: Houghton Mifflin Co., 1890.

Torrey, Bradford. *Nature's Invitation*. Boston: Houghton Mifflin Co., 1904.

Torrey, Bradford. *The Clerk of the Woods*. Boston/New York: Houghton Mifflin Company, 1903.

Van Dyke, Henry. *Little Rivers*. New York: Charles Scribner's Sons, 1895.

Vergil. *Georgics*. Chicago: University of Chicago Press, 1956.

Voltaire (François Marie Arouet). *The Oxford Dictionary of Quotations*. New York: Oxford University Press, 1955.

Wallace, David Rains. *The Klamath Knot: Explanations of Myth and Evolution*. San

Francisco: Sierra Club Books, 1983.

Walton, Izaac. *The Compleat Angler*. Harrisburg, Pennsylvania: The Stackpole Company, 1953.

Waterton, Charles. *Wanderings in South America*. New York: Everyman's Library, J. M. Dent & Sons, Ltd., E. P. Dutton & Co., 1925.

Weeks, Edward A. *The Open Heart*. Boston: Little, Brown and Co., 1955.

Wheeler, William M. *Social Life Among the Insects*. New York: Harcourt, Brace & Co., 1923.

White, Gilbert. *The Natural History of Selborne*. New York: D. Appleton and Co., 1898.

Whitman, Walt(er). *Song of Myself, Leaves of Grass*. New York: Doubledav, Doran & Co., Inc., 1940.

Williams, Tennessee (Thomas Lanier Williams). *Esquire*. September, 1971.

Williamson, Henry. *The Lone Swallows and Other Essays of the Country Green*. New York: E. P. Dutton, 1926.

Wilson, Alexander. "Letter to William Bartram" from *American Ornithology or the Natural History of the Birds of the United States*. New York: Collins and Co., 1828.

Wilson, Alexander. *The American Treasury*. Edited by Clifton Fadiman. New York: Harper and Brothers, 1955.

Yutang, Lin. *On The Wisdom of America*. New York: John Day Company, 1950.

Zwinger, Ann H. *Run, River, Run: A Naturalist's Journey Down One of the Great Rivers of the West*. New York: Harper & Row, Inc., 1975.

Abbey, Edward	Author, Naturalist
Abbott, Charles C.	American Naturalist, Author, Physician
Adams, J. Donald	Book Columnist, New York Times
Alexander, Cecil Frances	English Poet
Allingham, William	English Poet
Aristotle	Greek Philosopher, Teacher, Author, Classifier of Animals
Audubon, John James	American Bird Artist, Naturalist, Author
Audubon, Maria R.	Granddaughter of John J. Audubon, Author
Balzac, Honore de	French Novelist
Bartholin, Thomas	Danish Scholar
Bartram, William	American Naturalist, Author
Bates, Henry Walter	English Naturalist, Explorer, Writer
Bates, Marston	American Biologist, Writer, Medical Ecologist
Beebe, Charles William	American Scientist, Ecologist, Writer, first winner of the John Burroughs Medal (1926)
Belt, Thomas	British Ecologist, Naturalist, Explorer, Writer
Beston, Henry	American Writer, Naturalist
Bible, Holy	
Blake, William	English Poet and Artist
Blanton, Smiley	American Author
Bolles, Frank	American Writer, Secretary of Harvard (1877), Naturalist
Borland, Hal	American Author, winner of the John Burroughs Medal (1968)
Browne, Sir Thomas	English Writer and Scholar, Physician
Browning, Robert	English Poet
Burgess, Anthony	English Author, Composer, Play Producer, Lecturer
Burnford, Sheila	Novelist, winner of the Lewis Carroll Shelf Award (1971)

Burroughs, John	American Naturalist, Author, Poet, Essayist
Chesterfield, Fourth Earl of (Philip Dormer Stanhope)	British Statesman, Author
Christensen, Clyde M.	Educator, Author, Professor of Plant Pathology
Churchill, Sir Winston (Leonard Spencer)	English Statesman, Author, Prime Minister of England, Eloquent Speaker, winner of the Nobel Prize for Literature (1953)
Coleridge, Samuel Taylor	English Poet and Critic
Coman, Dale Rex	American Pathologist, Educator, Author, Professor of Plant Pathology
Confucius	Chinese Political and Ethical Philosopher, Teacher
Cott, Hugh B.	Lecturer in Zoology and Strickland Curator, University of Cambridge
Coues, Elliott	American Physician, Ornithologist, Scientist Naturalist and Author
Cowper, William	English Pre-Romantic Poet, Best Known Poem, *The Task*
Darwin, Charles Robert	English Naturalist, Biologist, Evolutionist
Davis, Henry E.	American Sportsman, Lawyer, Naturalist
Davis, William T.	American Businessman, Naturalist, Amateur Entomologist, Author
Day, Jr., Clarence Shepard	American Writer of Humorous Books, Son of Clarence Day, Famous Lawyer
De la Mare, Walter	English Poet, Novelist and Anthologist, Romantic Writer
De Morgan, Augustus	English Writer
Devoe, Alan	American Naturalist, Nature Writer
Dickinson, Emily	American Poet
Dillard, Annie	American Writer, winner of Pulitzer Prize for general non-fiction (1975)
Dimnet, Ernest	French Abbé, Literary Critic, Biographer
Dobie, J. Frank	American Teacher, Historian, Folklorist of Southwest
Dodsley, Robert	English Poet, Playwriter
Donne, John	English Poet, Clergyman
Edman, Irwin	American Philosopher, Professor of Philosophy, Poet

Edwards, Jonathan	New England Clergyman, Philosopher, Preacher, Revivalist in Colonial America
Eiseley, Loren	Author, Poet, Anthropologist, winner of the John Burroughs Medal (1961)
Ellwanger, George H.	Author
Emerson, Ralph Waldo	American Essayist, Poet, Philosopher, Lecturer
Euripides	Greek Tragic Playwright
Evans, Howard Signal	American Entomologist, Author, Educator, Professor of Entomology
Fabre, Jean Henri	French Entomologist, Author
Fadiman, Clifton	Writer, Editor, TV Entertainer
Fisher, James	English Ornithologist, Author, Educator
Flagler, Henry Morrison	American Builder of Florida Railroad and Resort Hotels
Gary, Romain	Russian-born French Novelist and Diplomat
Gay, John	English Poet and Playwright, Satirist
Grey, Edward	Viscount Grey of Fallodon, British Diplomat, Statesman, Author, Birding Enthusiast
Hagen, Walter	Great American Golfer and Champion
Halle, Jr., Louis	American Author, Educator, Naturalist, winner of the John Burroughs Medal (1941)
Harris, Sydney J.	American Newspaper Columnist
Heinrich, Bernd	American Biologist, Writer
Hoagland, Edward	American Author
Hubbard, Harlan	Musician, Writer
Hudson, William Henry	English Naturalist, Nature Writer, Novelist,
Hull, Cordell	American Statesman, winner of the Nobel Prize for Peace (1945), Secretary of State (1933-1944)
Huxley, Julian	English Biologist, Writer, Lecturer, Evolutionist and Scholar
Huxley, Thomas	English Biologist, Teacher, Popularizer of Science, Defender of Darwin's Theory of Evolution
Jackson, Holbrook	English Literary Scholar and Editor, Author
Jefferies, Richard	English Naturalist, Novelist
Johnson, Samuel	English Lexicographer, Essayist, Poet, Moralist

Keats, John	English Poet
Kempis, Thomas à (Thomas Hamerken Von Kempen)	German Monk and Writer, Author of *Imitation of Christ*
Kieran, John	American Naturalist, Nature Writer, Columnist, Ornithologist, winner of the John Burroughs Medal (1960)
Kilham, Lawrence	Writer-naturalist, winner of the John Burroughs Medal (1989)
Kipling, Rudyard	English Novelist, Poet, Short-story Writer
Krutch, Joseph Wood	American Critic, Essayist, Nature Writer, Teacher, winner of the John Burroughs Medal (1954)
Landis, Paul	Writer
Lawrence, Louise de Kiriline	Canadian Writer, Ornithologist, winner of the John Burroughs Medal (1969)
Le Gallienne, Richard	English Poet of French Descent
Leopold, Aldo	American Author, Essayist, Conservationist, Professor of Wildlife Management, winner of the John Burroughs Medal (1977)
Longfellow, Henry Wadsworth	American Poet, Romancer, Translator, College Professor
Longstreth, T. Morris	American Author, Popularizer of Books about Weather
Lopez, Barry	American Author, Naturalist, winner of the John Burroughs Medal (1979)
Lorenz, Konrad Z.	Austrian Ethologist or Animal Behavorist, Author, winner of the Nobel Prize for Physiology and Medicine (1973)
Lucretius (Titus Lucretius Carus)	Roman Poet
Macleod, Fiona (William Sharp)	English Writer
Maeterlinck, Maurice	Belgian Poet, Dramatist, Essayist, winner of the Nobel Prize for Literature (1911)
Marcus Aurelius	Roman Emperor, Author, Devoted to Stoic Philosophy

Matthiessen, Peter	American Author, Explorer, Naturalist, winner of the John Burroughs Medal (1982)
Mills, Enos Abijah	American Naturalist, Author, Conservationist
Milne, Lorus J. and Margery	Professors, Scientists, Photographers, Lecturers
Momaday, N. Scott	Native American, winner of a Pulitzer Prize (1969)
Montaigne, Michel de	French Author, Moralist, Creator of the Personal Essay
Muir, John	Scottish-born American Naturalist, Writer, Wilderness Preservationist
Murphy, Robert C.	American Ornithologist, Naturalist, Writer, Explorer, winner of the John Burroughs Medal (1938)
Olson, Sigurd F.	American Author, Naturalist, winner of the John Burroughs Medal (1974)
Paton, Alan	South African Novelist, Humanitarian Worker
Peattie, Donald Culross	American Author, Essayist, Botanist
Peterson, Roger Tory	American Ornithologist, Bird Artist, Author, Originator of Famous Peterson Nature Guides, winner of the John Burroughs Medal (1950)
Rickett, Harold William	American Author of Books about Wildflowers; Member, New York Botanical Gardens
Roosevelt, Theodore	Twenty-sixth President of the United States, Outstanding Field Naturalist, Explorer, Conservationist
Ruskin, John	English Writer and Critic, Stylist, Lecturer
Sa'di (Musharrif-Uddin)	Persian Poet
Sass, Herbert Ravenel	American Nature Writer, Regional Author of South
Schopenhauer, Arthur	German Philosopher, Author
Schweitzer, Albert	Alsatian Philosopher, Author, Musician, Theologian, Medical Missionary
Scott, Robert Falcon	English Antarctic Explorer, Naval Officer, Father of Peter Scott, English Ornithologist, Bird Painter and Writer
Sears, Paul Bigelow	American Botanist, Teacher, Conservationist, Ecologist, Author

Shakespeare, William	English Poet, Playwright, Actor
Shapley, Harlow	American Astronomer, Professor of Astronomy at Harvard University, Director of Observatory
Sharp, Dallas Lore	American Naturalist, Nature Writer, Educator
Skutch, Alexander Frank	American Naturalist, Specialist in Tropical American Ornithology, Author, winner of the John Burroughs Medal (1983)
Stanwell-Fletcher, Theodora C.	Naturalist, Writer, winner of the John Burroughs Medal (1948)
Steinhart, Peter	Author, Columnist with *Audubon* magazine
Stephens, James	Irish Poet and Fiction Writer
Stringer, Arthur	American Poet
Sutras	Ancient Hindu Aphoristic Manuals, possibly written 500-200 B.C.
Sutton, George M.	American Ornithologist, Bird Artist, Explorer, Educator, Curator of Ornithology, Author, winner of the John Burroughs Medal (1962)
Taylor, Walter P. Educator	American Biologist, Mammalogist, Author,
Teal, John and Mildred	American Writers, Scientists
Teale, Edwin Way	American Writer, Naturalist, Photographer, Amateur Entomologist, Scholar, winner of the John Burroughs Medal (1943)
Tennyson, Alfred Lord	English Poet
Terres, John K.	American Writer, Naturalist, Ornithologist, winner of the John Burroughs Medal (1971)
Thompson, Francis	English Poet
Thoreau, Henry David	American Essayist, Philosopher, Poet, Naturalist
Torrey, Bradford	American Naturalist, Ornithologist, Author
Van Dyke, Henry	American Clergyman, Educator, Novelist, Essayist, Poet, Author
Vergil (Publius Vergilius Maro)	Roman Poet, Philosopher
Voltaire (François Marie Arouet)	French Satirist, Philosopher, Historian, Dramatist

Wallace, David Rains	American Author, Naturalist, winner of the John Burroughs Medal (1984)
Walton, Izaac	English Author, Famous for Classic on Fishing, *The Compleat Angler*
Waterton, Charles	British Naturalist, Explorer, Writer
Weeks, Edward A.	American Editor, Writer
Wheeler, William M.	American Entomologist, Author
White, Gilbert	English Clergyman, Naturalist
Whitman, Walt(er)	American Poet, Journalist, Essayist
Williams, Tennessee (Thomas Lanier Williams)	American Playwright and Writer of Fiction
Williamson, Henry	English Novelist and Nature Writer
Wilson, Alexander	Scottish Immigrant, Pioneering American Ornithologist, Bird Artist, called "Father of American Ornithology"
Wilson, Woodrow	Twenty-eighth President of the United States, Scholar, Educator, President of Princeton University (1902-1910)
Yutang, Lin	Chinese Teacher, Editor, Writer
Zwinger, Ann	American Writer, Artist, winner of the John Burroughs Medal (1976)

T I T L E   I N D E X

grasshoppers 18, 85, 140
grasslands 155
Greeks 113
grief 216
grouse 40, 127
guidance 67
guilt 78
gulls 31, 236
guns 76, 98

habitat 183
habits 55, 139, 141, 180
happiness 25, 37, 50, 60, 103, 113, 200, 241
harbingers 134
hardship 159
harmony 183
harvest 10, 36, 63, 81, 83, 131, 151, 206
hate 126, 129, 194
hawks 40, 88, 116, 132, 140, 167, 174, 175, 239
health 213
hearing 23, 37, 56, 185, 214
heart 10, 35, 37, 106, 109, 150, 161, 175, 178, 186,
    218, 219, 238, 239
heaven 21, 33, 34, 46, 168
hedgehog 163
hell 113
herbs 206
herdsman 122
heritage 155
heros 24
herons 64, 99
herring gulls 31
hierarchy 134
hillsides 41, 107
history 193
hogs 231
homage 46
homeland 45
hope 3, 33, 72
horizon 6, 29, 153
hornworms 84
horses 107, 126, 210, 230
hostility 152, 158, 180, 190
houses 21, 32, 69, 131, 204
huckleberries 204
humanity 13, 27, 28, 29, 126, 163, 198, 217

hummingbirds 55, 171
hunger 28, 62, 68, 124, 168, 226, 229
hunted 10
hunters 62, 63, 118, 122
hunting 51, 118, 120, 232
hurricanes 122, 159, 183
hyena 135

ice 115, 122
idealism 44
idealists 44
ideas 58, 141
idleness 10, 60
ignorance 112, 141
illness 209
illusion 140, 151, 158, 226
illustration 59
imagination 25, 43, 72, 89, 218
imitation 127, 128
immortality 36, 99, 142, 206, 226
impala 136
impartiality 129
imperfections 25
impressions 17, 30, 185
improvement 214
impulses 13, 67, 128, 193
impurity 36
inadequacy 25
incipient 54
incubation 228
independence 209, 230
indifference 48
indiscretion 214
individuality 7, 8, 213
infinity 44, 242
influences 53
information 58, 196
inhabitants 14, 207
inheritance 208
inhumanity 193
innocence 70, 151, 181, 203, 205
insanity 212
insects 2, 20, 22, 24, 26, 84, 85, 86, 105, 110, 112,
    193, 194, 196, 226, 229, 230, 237
insight 190
inspiring 17, 36

John K. Terres is the author, co-author and editor of more than fifty books on natural history, including the benchmark reference, *Audubon Society Encyclopedia of North American Birds*, and the award-winning (John Burroughs Medal) *From Laurel Hill to Siler's Bog: The Walking Adventures of a Naturalist*.

Terres's bestselling title, *Songbirds in Your Garden*, was recently published in its third edition. In addition to writing *The Wonders I See*, *Flashing Wings: The Drama of Bird Flight* and *The Audubon Book of True Nature Stories*, he was the editor-in-chief of the twelve-volume *Audubon Nature Encyclopedia* and originator and editor of *The Living World Books*, an illustrated thirty-two volume series.

He is now a contributing editor for *National Wildlife*, *Bird Watcher's Digest* and *The Birder's World* and, for twelve years, was the editor for *Audubon Magazine*.